THE BAT-TLE OF BUN-KER HILL.

A CHILD'S HISTORY OF THE BATTLES OF AMERICA

Book 3

Illustrated

TOLD IN ONE-SYLLABLE WORDS

By Josephine Pollard
Published 1889
Re-published 1998; protected

Published By
Mantle Ministries
228 Still Ridge, Bulverde, Texas 78163

PREFACE.

The author has tried to tell the story of the *American Battles* so simply that the young reader will know just how, when, and where they were fought, and will feel as if with the troops in the camp and on the field. Some of the sea-fights will be found more fully described in "*Our Naval Heroes*," a book published by McLoughlin Brothers.

J. P.

CONTENTS.

CHAPTER I.
PAGE
LEXINGTON 1

CHAPTER II.
BUNKER HILL 17

CHAPTER III.
LONG ISLAND 31

CHAPTER IV.
TRENTON 41

CHAPTER V.
MONMOUTH COURT-HOUSE 50

CHAPTER VI.
A TRAITOR IN THE CAMP 56

CHAPTER VII.
YORKTOWN 66

CHAPTER VIII.
THE WAR OF 1812 75

CHAPTER IX.
LUNDY'S LANE 85

CHAPTER X.
IN MEXICO 93

CHAPTER XI.
Wars with the Indians 102

CHAPTER XII.
Bull Run 134

CHAPTER XIII.
Fort Donelson 148

CHAPTER XIV.
Shiloh 158

CHAPTER XV.
Antietam 165

CHAPTER XVI.
Vicksburg 174

CHAPTER XVII.
Gettysburg 185

CHAPTER XVIII.
Lookout Mountain 195

CHAPTER XIX.
In the Wilderness 204

CHAPTER XX.
Atlanta 207

CHAPTER XXI.
With Sheridan 214

CHAPTER XXII.
Petersburg 221

The Battles of America.

CHAPTER I.

LEXINGTON: APRIL 19, 1775.

IN the year 1620 a band of brave men and wom-en, called Pu-ri-tans, left Eng-land, the Old World, and came to A-mer-i-ca, the New World, where they might be free to serve God as they chose. They had heard a great deal of this New World, and thought to dwell there in peace for the rest of their days. But they came to shore on a cold, bleak coast, at the north-east end of the large stretch of land, and here, with but few tools to work with, and scant food to eat, they built their homes, and made the best that they could of their hard fate.

That part of the New World had for some time been known as New Eng-land, and those who made their

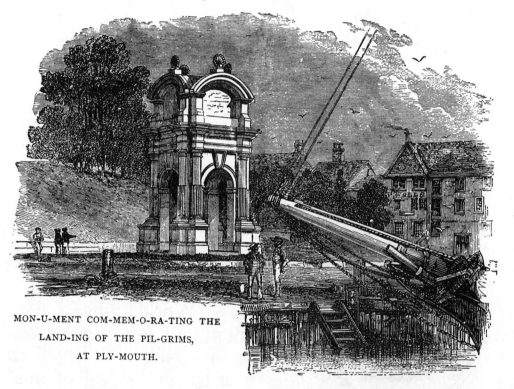

MON-U-MENT COM-MEM-O-RA-TING THE
LAND-ING OF THE PIL-GRIMS,
AT PLY-MOUTH.

homes there were still true to the old flag, and to the King who sat on the throne.

The red men thought that they had the first and best right to the land on which they had dwelt for so long a time. It was their own, and woe to the pale face who would try to wrest it from their hands.

But man has to fight his way through the world,

from the time he comes in-to it till he goes out of it; not all the while with guns and fire-arms, but in ways that tend to make the nerves strong, and the heart brave and true. These white men put their trust in God, and he gave them strength, and did not let hope die out of their hearts.

AN IN-DIAN VIL-LAGE.

They had fierce fights with the red men, and much blood was shed, their homes were set on fire, their wives and babes torn from their arms, and no one's life was safe.

But as the years went on new homes were built, farms spread out, and towns sprang up here and there, the chief one of which was Bos-ton. Here there was a fine bay, and to and from this port, ships came and went, and a large trade was kept up be-tween the Old World and the New.

GEORGE III.

The French who dwelt in Can-a-da were loath to have Eng-land take so much of the wealth of the New World, and wars with them and with the red men were kept up for a long term of years.

In 1768, Brit-ish troops were placed in Bos-ton to guard the town, and to see that no one broke the King's laws. These red-coats were harsh at times, and did so much to vex the A-mer-i-cans that they looked on them as the worst kind of foes.

In the year 1774, George the Third, then King of Eng-land, sought to gain more pow-er in the New World, and to make A-mer-i-cans the slaves of his will. His acts were such as to rouse the fierce hate

COM-MIS-SION-ERS LAND-ING AT BOS-TON.

of free men, and to put an end to all thoughts of peace and good-will.

Brit-ish troops were sent to Bos-ton to guard the ports so that no ships should land with tea, or goods

SAMU-EL AD-AMS.

that did not bear the King's stamp. The A-mer-i-cans would not pay the tax the King put on these things and made up their minds to do with-out tea, and all high-priced goods.

Soon food grew scarce, and rich and poor felt the scourge of the harsh task-mas-ter. Gen-er-al Gage was warned from time to time that if such harsh acts were kept up there would soon be war. But he felt no fear, as he thought that his well-trained troops would be more than a match for these raw Yan-kees.

Soon was heard the sound of fife and drums, and young and old, fa-thers and sons, took part each day in the drills that were to teach them how to hold and fire their guns, and how to keep step in the line of march.

Each win-ter the Bos-ton boys had found it great sport to build mounds of snow on the large Park, or Com-mon, which was their play-ground. These snow-hills the troops would beat down, just to vex the boys, who could stand it once or twice. But when this sort of thing was kept up, the boys were full of wrath, and made up their minds that Gen-er-al Gage should hear of it.

So they put on a bold front, and when they came near Gen-er-al Gage, a tall boy left their ranks and said to him, "We come, sir, to ask you to give us our rights."

"What!" said Gage, "have your fa-thers taught you this, and sent you out to show your-selves off?"

"No one sent us here, sir," said the boy, with a flash in his eyes that told of the scorn in his heart. "We have done no harm at all to your troops, but they trod down our snow-hills and broke up the ice on the ponds where we skate. We found fault, and they called us young reb-els, and told us to help our-selves if we could. We told the cap-tain of this, and he laughed at us as if he thought it a good joke. It is no joke to us, sir. For the third time our works have been torn down, and we will bear it no longer."

JOHN HAN-COCK.

Gage felt his heart stir with pride at the sight of such brave boys, and he told them that the troops should do no more harm to their play-grounds. Then he turned to an of-fi-cer near, and said, "Why, e-ven the chil-dren here draw in a love of free-dom with the air they breathe."

Though the Brit-ish were strict and stern, the Yan-kees were sharp and sly, and made use of all sorts of tricks to get the can-non balls, powder, and guns out of Bos-ton, that they might fit out a force of 15,000 men.

At length word was brought to Gen-er-al Gage that a large stock of guns and war-goods was hid at Con-cord, a town less than a score of miles from Bos-ton. On the night of A-pril 18, 1775, he sent 800 of his troops to Con-cord to seize them, and to tear down or burn the house where they were stored. These troops were in charge of Col-o-nel Smith and Ma-jor Pit-cairn. As soon as the Yan-kees in Bos-ton found where and why the red-coats had gone, they at once sent word to Ad-ams and Han-cock, two of their chief men, to be on their guard. Men were sent here and there to spread the news and sound the call "To arms! To arms! The foe is on us!" The name of one of these men was Paul Re-vere, and he rode at break-neck speed up hill and

PRO-VIN-CIALS AT CON-CORD.

down dale, till he came to Lex-ing-ton, a town on the road to Con-cord, and was the first to tell that the Brit-ish were to march that way.

Bells were rung, and guns were fired to rouse those to arms who dwelt on the hills and plains a-round.

"TO ARMS! TO ARMS!"

Men left their ploughs in the fields, seized their guns, and made haste to join the band that had sworn to free them-selves from the yoke of King George III.

As soon as Smith heard the fire of the guns, he called out part of his troops and told them to go to Lex-ing-ton as fast as they could run and seize the

PAUL RE-VERE.

bridg-es there. It was five o'clock on the morn of A-pril 19 when they reached the place, and the word soon spread, and three-score and ten Yan-kee troops at once took their place on the green near the road.

THE SKIR-MISH AT CON-CORD.

Ma-jor Pit-cairn, who was at the head of the Brit-ish troops, bade the Yan-kees lay down their guns and go back to their homes. When this was not done, he sprang from the ranks, drew forth his sword, and cried out to his men to fire.

CHARLES-TOWN. *(From an Old Print.)*

The troops with loud cheers ran up the road, and fired their guns at the Yan-kees, some of whom were killed, and not a few had quite bad wounds. Then Smith came up, and the Brit-ish troops moved on to Con-cord, which is four miles from Lex-ing-ton. Their first act was to spike the big field-guns, and to break up the wood-work so that they would be of no use.

To spike a gun is to drive a spike or nail into the hole on top, so that it can-not be set off. They then threw 500 pounds of bul-lets in-to the streams and wells, and spoiled all the flour and food of all sorts that they could lay their hands on.

While these deeds went on more and more Yan-kees came in by all the roads, un-til quite a crowd was on hand. Some of the Brit-ish that had been sent out to scour the land round a-bout Con-cord fell in with them and were forced to turn back to the main band of troops. As they came in the town of Con-cord a fight took place in which a large force of men were slain on both sides.

The Brit-ish found it much too hot for them in Con-cord, and made haste to march back to Lex-ing-ton. When they came to this place they were so worn out that the Yan-kees might have done with them as they chose, but for the aid — in the shape of fresh troops — that came to them just in the nick of time. As soon as

Battle of Lexington. 15

the worn-out troops had had the rest they were so much in need of, the whole force of the Brit-ish took up the line of march to Bos-ton, with two field-guns in the rear to keep back the Yan-kees, who sprang up thick and fast, and fired at them from all sides. A stone-wall or e-ven hedge would hide these sharp-shoot-ers, who had a good chance to pick their men, and wound if they did not kill these foes of free-men. We may be sure that the Brit-ish were glad when at sun-set they had reached Charles-town, for the day

BRIT-ISH GREN-A-DIER.   A-MER-I-CAN RI-FLE-MAN.

had been a hard one, and they had had poor luck. The next morn they were in Bos-ton.

In the fight at Lex-ing-ton 65 of the Brit-ish were slain and 180 had bad wounds to nurse. The A-mer-i-cans had 50 killed, and 38 with wounds made by Brit-ish guns.

It was a great blow to the Eng-lish; and oh! how

BAT-TLE OF LEX-ING TON.

it hurt their pride to think that the King's troops—so well-dressed and well-trained—had to give way be-fore such a "flock of Yan-kees" in home-spun suits, and with no skill in the art of war! But these ill-clad

Yan-kees "fought like brave men, one and all," and with a dash that seems born in an A-mer-i-can, and in the fight at Lex-ing-ton they found out what they could do, and it put new strength and hope in their hearts.

<blockquote>
Firm in the right, they took their stand
To drive the foe-men from their land.
</blockquote>

CHAPTER II.

BUNKER HILL: JUNE 17, 1775.

LORD HOWE.

At the close of May there were 10,000 red-coats in Bos-ton. With the fresh troops from Eng-land came Gen-er-als Howe, Clin-ton, and Bur-goyne, who had great skill in the art of war, and had won much fame for them-selves and their King on fields of strife.

The A-mer-i-cans had 16,000 men, with Gen-er-al

Ward at their head, and this force was spread out so that the British were quite shut in on the land side. The Yan-kees had thrown up a few breast-works here and there, and guards were placed at all points on the roads as far out as Cam-bridge.

There were three hills near Bos-ton from whose

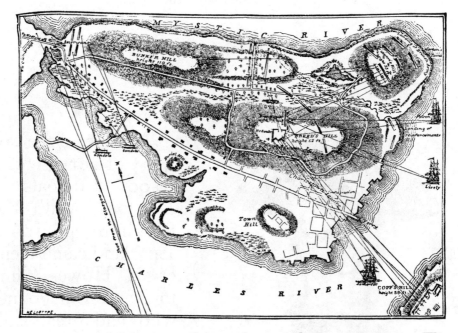

tops one could get a fine view of the town. They were known as Bun-ker Hill, Breed's Hill, and Copp's Hill.

It was made known to the A-mer-i-cans that on the night of June 18, the Brit-ish would march out and take their stand on Bun-ker Hill, near Charles-town, and on Dor-ches-ter Heights, south of Bos-ton. From both these points they could bring their guns to

THE DE-FENCE OF BREED'S HILL: PRES-COTT IN THE RE-DOUBT.

bear on the town, and so keep the Yan-kees out of it. The A-mer-i-cans made up their minds to put a stop to this fine plan, so on the night of June 16th Col-o-nel (*Ker-nel*) Pres-cott, with 1000 men and two field-guns, set out for Bun-ker Hill, where they were to build earth-works and make it an A-mer-i-can strong-hold.

For some cause these troops did not stop at Bun-ker Hill, but went on and up Breed's Hill, which was quite near Bos-ton, and brought them in range of the town and of the ships of war in the bay. All night they kept at work with pick-axe and spade, but in such a hush that not a sound was heard by those on guard in the town, and by day-light a strong fort loomed up on the hill-top, where when the sun last set there had been naught but green grass.

It was first seen at four o'clock in the morn-ing by the cap-tain of one of the ships of war, who at once be-gan to play up-on the A-mer-i-cans with his can-non. The noise woke up the whole town of Bos-ton, and the folks there — Brit-ish and Yan-kees — could scarce be-lieve their eyes when they saw what had been done in the few brief hours of the night.

Gen-e-ral Gage saw at once that if the A-mer-i-cans had a strong-hold on Breed's Hill they would soon drive him and his troops from the town, so he placed six of his large field-guns on Copp's Hill, and from there sent a storm of shot and shell at the A-mer-i-cans,

Battle of Bunker Hill.

which failed to do them much harm. Some of the guns of the fleet fired at them al-so, but still they kept on at their task and built up the fort — or *re-doubt* — which is the right name for that kind of earth-works. At noon the red-coats, 3000 strong, led by Gen-er-al Howe, went in boats to Charles-town to storm the earth-works there. They found the fort so strong, that Howe thought it best to wait for more troops. At this time the A-mer-i-cans had a chance to add one more to their force, a Doc-tor Jo-seph War-ren, whom they at once made Ma-jor-Gen-er-al.

JO-SEPH WAR-REN.

Gen-er-al Put-nam was the chief one in com-mand and went back and forth a-long the lines with words of help and cheer.

Crowds swarm on the hill-tops, on church-spires

and roofs, and wait and watch with hearts full of dread to see the fight be-gin.

At one o'clock the Brit-ish moved in two lines on the Amer-i-cans in Charles-town and drove them back, for they were in fear that they might be cut off from the main force of troops.

At a word from Gen-er-al Gage Charles-town was set on fire; the flames spread, and soon there was not a house left in the whole place. This act, for which there was no need, cast a gloom o-ver the A-mer-i-cans, and made the fierce fires of hate glow with more warmth in their breasts.

The dense smoke from Charles-town filled the air, and hung like a veil be-tween the A-mer-i-cans and the Brit-ish. The red-coats hoped the smoke would hide them so that they could rush up to the breast-works, scale them, and drive the Yan-kees out at the point of their guns.

But a breeze came up out of the west — the first that had been felt that day — and swept the smoke sea-ward, and left the Brit-ish troops in full view of the A-mer-i-cans.

The Brit-ish, borne down with the weight of their knap-sacks and the heat of the sun, moved up the slope of Breed's Hill at a slow pace. Gen-er-al Howe had charge of the right wing, Gen-er-al Pig-ot of the left.

All was still in the re-doubt, and but few men

could be seen by the red-coats on their way up the heights; but with-in the breast-works, and on the hills at the rear, 500 A-mer-i-cans lay hid, and at a sign from their chief would spring up in haste and fall up-on the foe. As they had no shot to waste, Pres-cott told them not to fire un-til the Brit-ish were so near that the whites of their eyes could be seen. "Then," he said, "aim at their waist-bands, and be sure to pick off those in com-mand who wear the hand-some coats."

At length, when the foe came to the right place, Pres-cott drew his sword, waved it on high, and at the shout of *Fire!* the A-mer-i-cans poured their shot in-to the ranks of the British and cut them down as the scythe cuts the grass in the field. This was kept up un-til the Brit-ish gave way and fled back to their boats. Few troops could be brought to Breed's Hill ere the next at-tack was made. The Brit-ish troops marched on the re-doubt in the same way they had done at first with Gen-er-al Howe in the van; for he had said to his men, "If the foe will not come out of their strong-holds we must drive them out, or else the town of Bos-ton will be set on fire by them. I shall not ask one of you to go a step fur-ther than where I go my-self at your head."

It took Gen-er-al Howe so long to bring up his troops for the third at-tack that the A-mer-i-cans had a chance to rest from the toils of the day. Their small stock of pow-der and ball was well nigh spent, and most of their mus-kets were the old flint-locks that had no points of steel. But the men made up their minds to use their guns as clubs when the pow-der gave out, if need be to fire stones, in place of shot, and to fight with a will as long as there was a ray of hope to cheer them on.

Put-nam in the mean time had to form the troops on Bun-ker Hill, and get fresh corps in by way of the strip of land, known as The Neck, which was be-tween the Mys-tic and the Charles Riv-ers. The Brit-ish had their ships of war in both these streams, and kept up such a fire that Put-nam had hard work to get his troops past this nar-row cause-way.

Gen-er-al Howe had found out a weak point be-tween the breast-works and the rail fence, and there he meant to lead the left wing with the field-guns, while a show of at-tack was made on the oth-er side. It was quite late in the day when the Brit-ish troops set out, and as they came up the hill they swept the breast-work with their guns, from end to end, and not a few of the A-mer-i-cans were slain. Those that were left went back in-to the re-doubt, from whence they made each shot tell. Gen-er-al Howe had a wound in his foot, but still fought at the head of his men, and led them on un-til but a bridge of earth was be-tween them and their Yan-kee foes. This they scaled, and

DEATH OF MA-JOR PIT-CAIRN.

the first man to leap on top of the wall was met with a show-er of stones, which must have scared him more than would the shot of a gun.

Ma-jor Pit-cairn, who led the troops at Lex-ing-ton, sprang up on the wall, and was shot at by a black man, who gave him his death-wound. Hand to hand the foe-men fought, but so large was the force of Brit-ish troops that the A-mer-i-cans had to leave the re-doubt, and yet so loath were they to give up the fight that some of them went back-wards and dealt hard blows right and left with their gun-stocks.

War-ren was the last man that left the works, and when not far from them, on the way to Bun-ker Hill, he was shot through the head and fell dead at once. The A-mer-i-cans at the rail fence had stood firm up to this time, and kept back the Brit-ish who sought to turn their flank. But when they saw the troops with their chief in flight from the fort, they too fled from the foe and thought the day was lost. In vain did Put-nam run back and forth like a mad-man, and cry out to them, "Make a stand here! We can stop them yet! In God's name, fire, and give them one shot more!" The whole force went pell-mell a-cross The Neck, and not a few of them were slain by the guns from the Brit-ish ships at that point. The Brit-ish troops were too worn out to keep up the chase so lay on their arms all night on Bun-ker Hill, while the A-mer-i-cans did the same on Pros-pect Hill, a mile off. Two Brit-ish field-guns played on them, but did slight harm, and as both sides felt loath to go on with the fight they had kept up for two hours, it now came to an end, and there was peace for a while.

It was a drawn fight; that is, neither side could claim to have won it; and, though there were brave deeds done on Bun-ker Hill and much blood shed, it was on Breed's Hill the chief scenes took place. The A-mer-i-cans lost 450 men. The Brit-ish loss was 1000; a large part of whom were men of high rank. The death of War-ren was a great blow to the A-mer-i-cans; and at the close of the war a mon-u-ment was put up on the spot where he fell. It stood

THE MON-U-MENT AT BUN-KER HILL.

for two-score years, and was torn down to make way for the tall shaft now known as Bun-ker Hill Mon-u-ment, which took near two-score years to build. The base is 30 feet square; and to reach the top you will have to climb 295 stone steps.

On Ju-ly 2, 1775, Gen-er-al George Wash-ing-ton came up from the South to take his place at the head of the A-mer-i-can troops, and to train them so that they would be less like a wild mob.

He found near 15,000 men in camp be-fore Bos-ton, where they held the Brit-ish in a state of siege. The Brit-ish troops did all the harm they could with their ships on the coast, and set fire to some of the small towns on the sea-port, but these acts put the Yan-kees more on their guard, and made them stand by their guns.

Then the cold win-ter set in, and the Brit-ish had hard work to find food to eat. Some of their store-ships were seized by the Yan-kees, and this they felt to be a great loss. On the morn of Feb-ru-a-ry 14, 1776, Gen-er-al Howe, who now led the red-coats in place of Gen-er-al Gage, sent some troops o-ver the ice to Dor-ches-ter Neck and burnt a few of the houses there.

Wash-ing-ton at once saw that his best plan was to march to Dor-ches-ter Heights, which are south of Bos-ton, and make this a strong-hold, so that the Brit-ish would be, as it were, be-tween two fires. So, on the night of March 4, a strong force of Yan-kees set out to cross Dor-ches-ter Neck, and as soon as they

THE MAS-SA-CRE AT BOS-TON.

reached the Heights, they went to work with a will to build the earth-works to screen them from the fire of Brit-ish guns.

This was no small task, as there was a thick coat of

ice on the ground, and the earth was frost-bound to a great depth. But Wash-ing-ton kept up such a fire with his field-guns at the north, that the noise of pick-axe and spade was not heard by the Brit-ish, and by day-light the A-mer-i-cans had built two forts on the Heights and made the place in-deed a strong-hold.

When Gen-er-al Howe saw these works, he said the A-mer-i-cans had done more in one night than the whole of his troops would have done in a month. He made up his mind to drive the Yan-kees from the Heights with the aid of his ships of war, and the fight was to take place the next day. But in the night a fierce storm came up that drove some of his ships a-shore on one of the isles, and the next day it rained so hard that the at-tack could not be made.

This gave the Yan-kees time to add to their strength, and the red-coats saw that it would be sure death for them to face so strong a force. They saw that they were caught in a trap, from which there was but one way to get out, and the Brit-ish troops and their friends were in great haste to quit the town.

They set sail March 17, 1776, and as the last of the Brit-ish went out of Bos-ton Gen-er-al Wash-ing-ton came in with his troops and was hailed with shouts of joy by those who were glad to be freed from Brit-ish rule, and with their own friends once more.

CHAPTER III.
LONG ISLAND: AUGUST 27, 1776.

When Gen-er-al Howe left Bos-ton it was thought that he meant to join the Brit-ish fleet then near New York. So the next day Wash-ing-ton sent five reg-i-ments, in charge of Gen-er-al Heath, to that

HAL-I-FAX.

town, and soon came up with all the rest of the troops, and at once set them to work to build forts at New York and on Long Isl-and.

Gen-er-al Howe had not gone to New York, but to Hal-i-fax, where he staid for some time to give his troops the rest they had need of, and that the sick ones might have a chance to gain their health and strength. As soon as all were well he set sail for the south, and on July 2, landed on Stat-en Isl-and with a force of 9000 men. His broth-er, Lord Howe, Ad-mi-ral of the Brit-ish fleet, soon came up with his ships of war fresh from Eng-land, on board of which were at least 20,000 men.

Wash-ing-ton's whole force was not more than 20,000, and his raw, ill-armed, ill-trained troops were a poor match for the well-drilled red-coats. But he made the best use that he could of the means that he had, and sent Gen-er-al Greene to Long Isl-and to cast up strong earth-works back of Brook-lyn. Greene soon fell sick, and Gen-er-al Sul-li-van took his place with Gen-er-al Put-nam chief in com-mand.

If you will look on a map of New York you will see that the shore of Stat-en Isl-and is quite near the shore of Long Isl-and. The space be-tween them is called The Nar-rows.

On Au-gust 22, 1776, Gen-er-al Howe, with 15,000 troops, crossed The Nar-rows and landed on Long Isl-and near Graves-end. There was a range of hills, thick with woods, from The Nar-rows to Ja-mai-ca, through which the roads ran here and there. Wash-ing-ton gave strict or-ders that guards were to be kept at all these roads; but Sul-li-van did not see the need of it, and did not stretch his lines out as far as he should have done. He saw his mis-take too late.

The A-mer-i-cans, 8000 strong, were in camp in Brook-lyn, just a-cross from New York. On their

GEN-E-RAL GREENE.

right flank was a long, low marsh, and on their left a bend in the East Riv-er, known as Wal-la-bout Bay. It was plain to be seen that the Brit-ish meant to gain the rear of the A-mer-i-cans by the Bed-ford and Ja-mai-ca roads, and 2500 men were at once put on guard at these points.

On Au-gust 26, the Brit-ish set out in charge of Sir Hen-ry Clin-ton and Lord Corn-wal-lis, and at three o'clock the next morn-ing word came to Put-nam that the Brit-ish had made their way through the pass near where Green-wood now is. Put-nam at once sent Stir-ling with a force of troops to drive them back. Near Gow-an-us Creek Stir-ling was met by a large force of red-coats, and in the Bay on his right flank were some of Howe's ships with well-armed men on board.

At the same time the Ger-mans in the pay of the Brit-ish were on their way to force the pass at a point to the east — where Pros-pect Park now is — while Howe, with the main force of the Brit-ish, led by Clin-ton and Corn-wal-lis, sought to gain the rear of the A-mer-i-cans through the Bed-ford pass.

The A-mer-i-cans stood firm, with their guns and their eyes fixed on the foe. From be-hind breast-work and tree they looked down, and felt no fear, when lo! the roar of guns in the rear of their left flew through the lines and told a tale of woe. The Brit-ish had turned their left flank, and they were be-tween two fires! While Sul-li-van tried to keep the Ger-mans at bay, Clin-ton had gained his rear and fell on him, and drove him back on the Ger-mans. There was a sharp hand-to-hand fight, and when Sul-li-van saw there was no chance for his men he bade them make haste for the camp while there was yet time.

It was too late! As they came out of the woods they were met by the guns of the Brit-ish, and when the A-mer-i-cans found there was no way out but through the ranks of the foe, they fought with skill and strength, and were most brave and bold. Some forced their way through to the camp, some fled to the woods, a large part of them were slain, and not a few fell in-to the hands of the foe. Sul-li-van was caught in a field of corn.

SIR HEN-RY CLIN-TON.

Stir-ling and his troops were the last of the A-mer-i-cans left in the field, and for four hours they fought the Brit-ish, whose force was much lar-ger than their own. No fresh troops came to their aid, and when the Brit-ish war-ships fired their guns at the fort at Red Hook in their rear, Stir-ling bade his troops flee for their lives.

The bridge at Gow-an-us Creek, near which they

fought, was in flames, and the men had to ford the creek, which was thick with mud. Lord Corn-wal-lis tried to stop their flight, but was held back by Lord Stir-ling, who fought with him till all the A-mer-i-cans had crossed but sev-en, who were drowned.

That night the A-mer-i-can camp was a scene of grief and woe, for they mourned the loss of dear friends, and knew not what was the fate of those who fell into the hands of the foe. It is said that Gen-er-al Wood-hull, who failed to guard the Bed-ford road, was seized by the Brit-ish on his way home, and cut to bits be-cause he would not say "God save the King."

The Brit-ish held the ground they had won, and spent the night in a mad sort of joy. The next day a fierce rain-storm set in, which kept A-mer-i-cans and Brit-ish in their own camps, and gave the worn-out men a chance to rest.

Wash-ing-ton had not slept for two days, and his mind was ill at ease, for he thought that Lord Howe would push on and at-tack the camp at Brook-lyn. This he did not do, but threw up earth-works near Fort Greene, and laid plans for a long siege. Fresh troops were sent to Wash-ing-ton from the north end of Man-hat-tan Isl-and, but even with these he could not hope to beat the Brit-ish, so he made up his mind to steal out of their clutch-es.

Battle of Long Island.

On the night of Au-gust 29, 1776, a thick fog hung o-ver New York Bay, through which not a glimpse could be seen of the Brit-ish fleet. And strong as was the Ad-mi-ral's spy-glass he could not make out the shore of New York, or tell what friend or foe was do-ing there.

In the A-mer-i-can camp, on Brook-lyn Heights, there was a hush and a stir that told that some great deed was to be done. The troops stole out and made haste to the fer-ry, and in boats that lay in wait for them crossed over the East Riv-er, and, be-ing hid by the dense fog, land-ed safe on the New York side.

MOUTH OF THE HUD-SON RIV-ER.

A wo-man who lived near the fer-ry, and knew what was going on, sent her black man to tell the Brit-ish of the flight of the A-mer-i-cans; but he came up to a Ger-man guard, who did not know a word that he said, and would not let him pass, so he had to turn back with his tale not told. On the morn of Au-gust 30, the Brit-ish pick-et — that is, the man on guard at a point far from the camp, or the main lines — saw no signs of life a-bout the A-mer-i-can lines. This was a strange thing, and he set off at once to find out the cause. He crept near the earth-works, peeped in the camp, and saw — no one. Then he gave a great shout, and the rest of the out-guards came up with a rush to seize the earth-works, and they saw in mid-stream, out of gun-shot, the last of the boats which had borne the A-mer-i-cans a-cross that night. In a small boat, or barge, there sat an A-mer-i-can of-fi-cer with a calm and proud mien, and a smile on his face that told of the joy he felt as a glance at the shore showed him that his troops were out of the reach of the foe. This was George Wash-ing-ton.

When Gen-er-al Howe found out what had been done, and how the game had slipped out of his hands, he swore a big oath, raised the Brit-ish flag in the camp on Brook-lyn Heights, and laid plans to seize New York with the A-mer-i-can troops in it.

In the mean-time the head men of the A-mer-i-cans sought to make peace with the foe, but Lord Howe did not like the terms, and the war went on.

On Sep-tem-ber 15, Gen-er-al Clin-ton, with 4000 men, crossed the East Riv-er in flat-boats, came on shore at Kipp's Bay, and took post on some high

GEORGE WASH-ING-TON.

ground a-bout five miles north of New York. The A-mer-i-cans set to guard that place were so scared by the noise of the guns from the ships-of-war, that they fled at sight of the foe and did not fire a shot. Wash-ing-ton met them on the road, drew his sword, and tried to bring them up in-to shape. But it was no use; and his ser-vant seized the reins of his horse and turned him away from the foe.

The rest of the Brit-ish troops soon joined those of Clin-ton, and fought their way through the A-mer-i-can ranks, and took New York. The A-mer-i-cans took their stand at Har-lem, nine miles off, but lest Gen-er-al Howe should hem them in, Wash-ing-ton moved his troops to King's-bridge, and so on from place to place as the Brit-ish drove them. His men were ill-armed, and worse clad, they had but few tents, and no pots or pans in which to cook their food, and would have stood no chance in a fight with so large a force as Howe had with him. So there was naught to do but to fall back and wait for fresh troops. The red-coats kept close at their heels, and fear spread through the land and peace seemed a long way off.

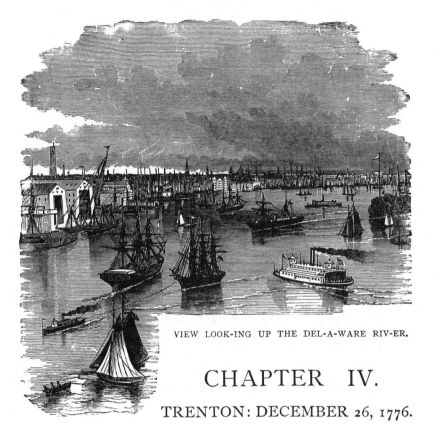
VIEW LOOK-ING UP THE DEL-A-WARE RIV-ER.

CHAPTER IV.

TRENTON: DECEMBER 26, 1776.

Win-ter had set in when Wash-ing-ton and his troops crossed the Del-a-ware, and it was no part of Gen-er-al Howe's plan to lead his men out to fight at such a time of the year, when ice and snow were on the ground. So he brought them to a halt at Tren-ton, and sent corps (*kors*) of Brit-ish troops to the towns near at hand, and as far off as Prince-ton, New Bruns-wick, and E-liz-a-beth town.

So sure was he that the war would soon be brought to an end, and the Brit-ish win the day, that he took no care to guard the weak points on the shore of the stream, and not a gun was to be seen there. For he had no thought that the reb-els, who for two months had kept up their flight, would dare to turn and face the foe from whom they fled.

The A-mer-i-cans were weighed down with a sense of gloom, and but for the brave heart of the Com-mand-er-in-chief, George Wash-ing-ton, all would have been lost. He would not yield to Brit-ish rule; he knew no such word as fail. He went here and there to rouse men to take up arms and drive the foe from the land, and by this means raised his force from 2000 to 6000 men. When he learned how far Gen-er-al Howe had stretched out his lines, Wash-ing-ton said, "Now is the time to clip their wings when they are so spread;" and at once be-gan a plan of at-tack.

Now the King's troops at Tren-ton were Ger-mans, in charge of Col-o-nel Rall, and Wash-ing-ton knew that they thought a great deal of Christ-mas, and would make much of the day, and keep up their feasts till a late hour. They would be off their guard, and that was the time for the A-mer-i-cans to pounce down up-on them.

A band of scouts on horse-back, who had been through Jer-sey and knew naught of Wash-ing-ton's

WASH-ING-TON CROSS-ING THE DEL-A-WARE.

scheme, came on the Ger-man camp at Tren-ton, and a few shots were fired from both sides. Rall had heard that an at-tack was to be made and thought that this was the whole of it, and so took his ease and kept Christ-mas with his friends in Ger-man style.

When night set in, Wash-ing-ton brought 2000 of his troops down to the shore of the Del-a-ware at a point five miles above Tren-ton, where they were to cross the stream, which was full of great lumps of ice. The tide was swift, the night was dark, and oh! so cold! and at mid-night a storm of snow and sleet set in.

But Wash-ing-ton kept on — boats were brought up in haste, and by day-light the troops stood in line of march on the New Jer-sey shore. They moved in two lines: one led by Sul-li-van, who was to keep the riv-er road; while the oth-er, with Wash-ing-ton at the head, took a road that led off to the left. The roads were a glare of ice in some parts, and the men could scarce keep their feet, yet in spite of all these ills the brave men kept on their way. It was eight o'clock when they reached Tren-ton, but so still had been their march that they were not seen nor heard till they came to the pick-et line on the edge of the town.

Then the sound of the guns woke Rall and his of-fi-cers from their deep sleep, and there was a great stir in the camp. Rall, who was a brave man, soon had his men un-der arms, and made a bold stand to meet and crush the reb-el foe. There was a sharp fight for half an hour, in the midst of which Col-o-nel Rall met with his death-wound and had to be borne from the field. His men found the fire of the A-mer-i-can guns so hot for them that a-bout 1000 threw down

VIEW OF WASH-ING-TON'S QUAR-TERS AT MOR-RIS-TOWN.

their arms and gave them-selves up as pris-on-ers, and the rest — most of whom were light horse-men — took to their heels. But few of the Ger-mans were killed, and the A-mer-i-cans lost but four or five men, some of whom froze to death that cold, cold night.

Wash-ing-ton and his troops crossed the Del-a-ware a-gain, and took with them the spoils they had won in the fight: 1000 Ger-mans, 1200 small-arms — that is, such fire-arms as are borne in the hand — six brass field-guns, and all the Ger-man flags, both large and small.

This was a great prize and sent a thrill of joy through the A-mer-i-cans, who had been cast down for so long a time. A fresh hope took hold of their hearts. They felt that there was a turn of the tide; and Wash-ing-ton, in whom they had great faith, was urged by some to push on and add to the fame he had won, and drive the Brit-ish from the land.

This he would have been glad to do, but it was thought best not to force a fight, but to wait and see what course the foe would take.

The Brit-ish troops in Jer-sey made raids on the farms and homes through the state, stole all they could lay their hands on, and by their acts drove the men to arms. Cheered by the news from Tren-ton, and stung by the harsh acts of the red-coats, those who had kept close at home and felt no call to fight now took down their guns and went forth with brave hearts to lay down their lives, if need be, to save the land they loved from Brit-ish rule.

Thus there was a great gain to the A-mer-i-can force, and in the year of 1777, e-lev-en bat-tles took place in the small state of New Jer-sey, some of which were won by the Brit-ish and some by the A-mer-i-cans.

In the month of June Gen-er-al Howe left New York with 30,000 men and took up his post at New Bruns-wick. Wash-ing-ton was at Mor-ris-town with less than 8000 men, and some of these not fit to take the field. Gen-er-al Howe sought to draw Wash-ing-ton out of his strong-hold and get him in a tight place where there would be more of a chance for the Brit-ish; but as Wash-ing-ton would not leave his camp, Howe went back and did all the harm that he could on his march to New Bruns-wick.

In Ju-ly Ad-mi-ral Howe brought his ships-of-war up the Del-a-ware, and Wash-ing-ton at once moved his troops to Phil-a-del-phia, to guard that town. Here a fierce fight took place, and Wash-ing-ton was forced to fall back as far as Ches-ter, eight miles from the Brit-ish lines.

Ben-ja-min Frank-lin, one of the great men of that time, and a stanch friend to A-mer-i-ca, was vexed at the good-will shown to the red-coats by a large part of the towns-folk, and said: "Howe did not take Phil-a-

IN-DE-PEND-ENCE HALL, PHIL-A-DEL-PHIA.

del-phia; Phil-a-del-phia took Howe." And the most of folks like to be on the side that wins.

Through the fall of the year Wash-ing-ton and his men were in camp at White-marsh, a fine stretch of low-land 14 miles from Phil-a-del-phia. Here they staid till De-cem-ber 11, 1777, when they set out for Val-ley Forge, a score of miles north of Phil-a-del-phia, as there they would be more safe from the foe, and could serve as a guard for the Con-gress, which had fled from Phil-a-del-phia, and was then at the town of York.

Such a march as that was! No pen can write —no brush can paint— no tongue can tell the woes of that brave band of 11,000 men, more than half of whom were not fit to be out of their beds.

The cold blast cut like a knife through the clothes that hung on their backs in rags. The ground was hard and

LA-FAY-ETTE.

rough for their bare feet, and they left a trail of blood to mark the path they trod to Val-ley Forge.

Here they had naught but rude log huts to live in, which they built them-selves, and which were but a poor screen from the rough winds, for these poor ill-clad, half-starved men.

At this time the Mar-quis de La-fay-ette—a young

man of great wealth — came from France to lend his aid to the A-mer-i-can cause. The news that the French king would send troops and lend what aid he could to A-mer-i-ca sent a thrill through the camp at Val-ley Forge. A day was set a-part in which to give thanks to God; guns were fired; shouts and cheers were heard and loud cries of "Long live the King of France!"

With New Year came good food and clothes, and good cheer to those at Val-ley Forge; and, as fresh troops had been sent to him, Wash-ing-ton broke up the camp, and on June 18 set out to chase the Brit-ish through New Jer-sey as soon as they should leave Phil-a-del-phia.

CHAPTER V.

MON-MOUTH COURT-HOUSE: JUNE 28, 1778.

The Brit-ish troops in Phil-a-del-phia had a grand good time, and were as gay as they could be, while those at the north, near Can-a-da, fought hard, with the red men to help them, to drive the A-mer-i-cans from their strong-holds on that line. Word came from Eng-land to push the work at the north, and at day-break of June 18, 1778, Gen-er-al Howe set out from Phil-a-del-phia to join the main force, which was to be led by Gen-er-al Bur-goyne. That night Howe and his men, 17,000 strong, went in-to camp at Cam-den, New Jer-sey.

As soon as Wash-ing-ton heard of their move, he broke up the camp at Val-ley Forge, and at once gave chase to the foe. It was Clin-ton's plan to march to New Bruns-wick, and go by boats from there to New York. But as soon as he found out that Wash-ing-ton was on his track, he turned at Al-len-town and took the road to Mon-mouth Court House, so as to make his way to San-dy Hook, and thence to New York by boats.

BUR-GOYNE.

Wash-ing-ton kept on a line with him, so as to strike him at the first chance. But Clin-ton did not wish to fight, for he was in no trim to meet a foe. He had charge of all the vans and the camp-stores, and there was with him a host of men who served the camp, so that his line was twelve miles in length. He set up his camp near the court-house in Free-hold, on June 27, and there Wash-ing-ton made up his mind to strike him, if he should move the next day, so that he could not reach Mid-dle-town Heights, which would give him a fine strong-hold.

Gen-er-al Charles Lee led the van of the A-mer-i-can troops. But he was not true to the cause, and had no wish to check Clin-ton's march through New Jer-sey, and found fault all the time.

When word came to Wash-ing-ton the next day — June 28 — a hot Sun-day — that Clin-ton was a-bout to move, he told Lee to fall on the rear of the Brit-ish and force them to fight. Lee seemed to have no plan of his own, and was so slow that he gave Clin-ton time to get his troops in line, and his orders were so queer that his gen-er-als sent word to Wash-ing-ton to come on the field at once, and with all his troops.

While Wayne led an at-tack that he was sure would go hard with the foe, Lee came up and urged him to draw back and make a feint at that point; that is, give them a scare and do them no harm. Just then Clin-ton changed front and sent a large force, on horse and on foot, to at-tack Wayne.

La-fay-ette, who thought there was now a good chance to gain the rear of the Brit-ish, rode up in haste to Lee and asked if he might not move on them. At first Lee said No; but when he saw how much the Mar-quis wished to go, he told him to wheel his troops to the right and strike Clin-ton's left. At the same time he sent some of Wayne's men off to give strength to the right; and erelong bade the whole of the right fall back, and the troops in his charge were soon in full flight, with the Brit-ish in hot chase.

GEN-ER-AL C. LEE.

Wash-ing-ton was on his way with the main force to aid Lee, when he was met with the news that the van-guard had turned back. Lee had sent him word of this, and if these troops came up on a run it would put the whole force to flight.

Wash-ing-ton was in a rage, and when he met Lee he rode up to him, and in a stern voice asked him the cause of this wild rout. Lee took no blame to him-self, and there was no time for a war of words. Wash-ing-ton wheeled his horse, and rode to the rear, and bade Os-wald take post on a hill near by with two large field-guns.

These guns, aimed with skill, soon held the foe in check. It roused the hearts of the troops to have Wash-ing-ton near them, and in a short time the flight was at an end.

The troops were then brought up on a height, where Stir-ling had placed a lot of can-non, with Gen-er-al Greene in com-mand on the right and Stir-ling on the left.

The two foes — the Brit-ish and the A-mer-i-cans — were now face to face. The Brit-ish, 7000 strong, were on a road in the midst of deep swamps. Their horse-men tried at first to turn the A-mer-i-cans' left flank, but were swept back, much to their shame. Then the troops on foot came up, and there was a sharp fight, in which all the guns, great and small, took part. For awhile there was doubt which side would win, when Gen-er-al Wayne came up with fresh troops and claimed the day for A-mer-i-ca. Col-o-nel Monck-ton saw at once that the Brit-ish might have a chance if they could get rid of Wayne, so he led his troops to a bay-o-net charge.

So fierce was Wayne's storm of bul-lets up-on them that all the Brit-ish of-fi-cers were slain, and the brave

Monck-ton fell at the head of his troops, as he waved his sword, and gave the shout to urge them on. His men then fell back to the heights where Lee had been in the morn-ing.

Night set in, and the worn-out troops—A-mer-i-cans and Brit-ish—lay down to rest, that they might have strength to go on with the fight as soon as day broke.

But at mid-night Clin-ton with-drew his troops through the deep sands of the roads, and was far on his way to San-dy Hook when the A-mer-i-cans first knew of his flight. Wash-ing-ton did not give chase, and so the red-coats made their way back to New York, with the loss of 1000 men, at least three score of whom had died from the heat. The A-mer-i-cans lost more than 50 men from the same cause. The whole loss of the A-mer-i-cans was 228. Wash-ing-ton took up his march north-ward, and went in-to camp at White Plains, New York, till late in the fall.

AN-THO-NY WAYNE.

All through the year 1779 war was rife at the North and the South, and fierce were the fights with the red men and the Brit-ish. As their foes gained ground, the hearts of the A-mer-i-cans were full of gloom, and yet they would not yield, nor join in the cry of "God save the King."

At the close of the year Sir Hen-ry Clin-ton left New York with 8000 troops, and some of the ships of the line, to make an at-tack on the states of the South, and to bring the war to an end as soon as he could. A storm drove the fleet out of its course, some of the ships were seized by the A-mer-i-cans, some lost at sea, and when he reached Sa-van-nah he was in poor trim, and had to stay there for some time.

The folks through the South were tired of war and longed for peace, and it was no hard task for Clin-ton to get men to join his side and take up arms for the Crown.

CHAPTER VI.

A TRAITOR IN THE CAMP.

In the spring of 1780 Wash-ing-ton saw there was need of more troops in the Car-o-li-nas, and a large force was sent there, with Gen-er-al Gates as their chief. Up to this time the A-mer-i-cans had stood on guard, and let the Brit-ish strike the first blow. But Gates made up his mind to push on and drive the

Brit-ish, in charge of Lord Raw-don, out of Cam-den and make them fall back on Charles-ton.

But Raw-don, as soon as he heard the A-mer-i-cans

GEN-E-RAL GATES.

were near, sent word to Lord Corn-wal-lis at Charles-ton, who made haste to join him.

On the night of Au-gust 15, the Brit-ish and A-mer-i-cans set out — one from the North and the oth-er from the South — but with no thought or plan as to where they would meet and form in line of battle. The two van-guards met near San-der's Creek, and began to fire in the dark. But both soon came to a halt, formed in line, ceased to fire, and lay in wait for the dawn. Then a fierce fight took place, and for awhile it was hard to tell which side would win.

The Brit-ish charged with fixed bay-o-nets, and soon put the Vir-gin-ia and Car-o-li-na troops to flight. The Ma-ry-land and Del-a-ware troops still fought on, and seemed as if they would win the day at last, for more than once they forced the British to fall back.

At length the whole force of the foe was brought to bear on these two corps, and a storm of bul-lets was poured in their ranks. At the same time Corn-wal-lis charged on them with fixed bay-o-nets, which made them give way, and as they broke Col-o-nel Tarle-ton's horse-men charged up-on them, and drove them from the field with great loss.

Gen-er-al Gates, with his troops that were left, fell back to a safe place, and had no more to do with the war. He was not thought fit to lead troops to fight and win, and so the brave Gen-er-al Greene was put in charge of the A-mer-i-can force at the South.

On the night be-fore the fight at San-der's Creek, Col-o-nel Sum-ter — from whom Fort Sum-ter takes its name — had been sent to rout the Brit-ish from their post on the Wa-ter-ee. He won the fight, and took two-score wag-ons, and one hun-dred pris-on-ers. While Sum-ter was on his way to join Gates, Col-o-nel Tarle-ton with his horse-men rode in-to the camp and found him quite off his guard. Sum-ter's men were worn out with hard work and loss of sleep, and had no strength to fight. Some were killed, some fled to to the woods and swamps to save them-selves, and Tarle-ton set the Eng-lish-men free and with great pride took them back to the Brit-ish camp.

When the Brit-ish left Phil-a-del-phia, in 1778, Wash-ing-ton placed Gen-er-al Ben-e-dict Ar-nold there with some troops, as chief man of the town. Ar-nold had a bad wound and could not take part in the fights, and he might

BEN-E-DICT R-NOLD.

have done good work for the cause had such been his choice. But, though a brave man, he was not good or true, and Wash-ing-ton could not trust him.

He lived in fine style, and made a great show; and those who knew him best did not think it strange when he took a wife from a-mong those who hoped for Brit-ish rule in A-mer-i-ca. These folks were known as To-ries.

At last Ar-nold was charged with fraud, and forced to leave his high place, and he at once went to the camp at Mor-ris-town, where Wash-ing-ton then was, to be tried for his crimes. He used all his arts to help his own cause, but in vain. His guilt was clear.

He was a proud man, and the shame he felt did not bow him to the dust, but roused in him a fierce hate for A-mer-i-ca and the cause once so dear to his heart.

His first step was to let the Brit-ish know of this change in his views, and he wrote to Sir Hen-ry Clin-ton of his plans. For a fixed price he was to sell the A-mer-i-cans to the Brit-ish, and none but a Ju-das could have done so base a deed.

Now there was a strong fort at West Point, which had been a great bar to the Brit-ish in their raids north-ward from New York. Ar-nold's pride would not let him join the Brit-ish ranks, so he made up his mind to go back to the A-mer-i-cans, get com-mand of West Point, and then give it up, with all its arms, troops, and stores, in-to the hands of the Brit-ish.

He had kept a fair face to the A-mer-i-cans, though his heart was full of hate, and when he asked for the com-mand of West Point they gave it to him, for there was great need of brave men. But Wash-ing-ton had doubts if he was the right man for the place, and kept a close watch on him for some time.

There was a young man named John An-dré, who held the rank of Ma-jor in the Brit-ish ar-my, on the

WASH-ING-TON AT WEST POINT.

staff of Gen-er-al Clin-ton. He was well known to Ar-nold, and was a brave youth, with a fine mind. He was drawn into the plot, and notes, in a feigned hand, passed back and forth be-tween the two, which they did not sign with their own names. Ar-nold took the name of *Gus-ta-vus*, and An-dré that of *An-der-son*.

Ar-nold made his home at the house of a man named Rob-in-son, who, though born in A-mer-i-ca, had joined the ranks of the Brit-ish, and to him the plot was made known, as there would be need of his aid.

MA-JOR AN-DRÉ.

As soon as Ar-nold thought Wash-ing-ton had left West Point for Hart-ford, where he had a call to go, he sent word to Clin-ton that he must see An-dré at once; for in-to his hands, and none but his, would he give the maps and pa-pers that Clin-ton would need ere he could take the fort. It was thought that this blow would end the war, and An-dré was glad to take a part in it that he thought would bring him great fame.

So on the night of Sep-tem-ber 19, 1780, he and Rob-in-son set forth on board the sloop-of-war *Vul-ture*, and the next morn-ing were at Fort Clin-ton, six miles south of West Point. They did not leave the boat un-til dark, and Ar-nold met them as they stepped on shore.

All the plans were laid be-fore An-dré, and Sep-tem-ber 25 was the day set on which Ar-nold would yield the forts in-to the hands of the Brit-ish.

An-dre set out at once for New York, to take the word to Clin-ton, but when he sought to go on board the *Vul-ture* he found that she had had to drop some miles be-low to get out of reach of the guns that were fired on her from the shore. The men in the row boat would not go down to the *Vul-ture*, and An-dré went back to Ar-nold. He took off his u-ni-form, and put on a suit of plain clothes, which were brought to him by a man named Smith, a friend to the Brit-ish, and set out by land to New York. Smith went with him part of the way, and as each had a pass signed by Ar-nold, they passed through the A-mer-i-can lines with-out harm. An-dré then put spurs to his horse, and dashed on to New York with great speed.

When near Tar-ry-town a man with a gun sprang from a clump of low trees by the road-side, seized the reins, and cried out, "Where are you bound?" At the same time two more men came up. An-dré thought they were Brit-ish, so did not show his pass, but asked them where they came from. "From be-low," said they. An-dré thought that this meant that they came from New York, and he said, "So do I. I am an Eng-lish of-fi-cer, and in great haste to get back to my post. So let me go on my way."

"You belong to our foes!" they cried. "You are now in our hands!"

They searched him, and found in his boots Ar-nold's maps and plans, which gave proof that they had caught a spy. André was struck dumb for a-while, and scarce knew what to do. Then he told the men they might have his horse, his purse, his watch, and that a large sum of gold would be sent to them from Eng-land, if they would let him go. But they would not; and he was borne by them to Col-o-nel Ja-mie-son, who was in charge of the out-posts.

Ja-mie-son, who had no thought but that Ar-nold was a true man, wrote him at once that one An-der-son, who bore a pass signed by him, had been seized on the road to New York.

Ar-nold was at break-fast when the news came to him, and it gave him a great shock. But there were still two days left ere Wash-ing-ton would be back, and he thought some-thing might be done in that time.

While lost in thought, word was brought him that Wash-ing-ton was near, and would soon be with him. He at once made haste to his wife's room, and cried out " All is found out! An-dré is a pris-on-er! Wash-ing-ton will soon know all! Burn all my pa-pers! I fly to New York!" He then kissed her and their child, rushed from the room, seized the horse of one of the of-fi-cers, and fled to the Hud-son, where he had a barge with men at the oars. He threw him-self in-to it, and in a short time was on board the *Vul-ture*.

An-dré was tried as a spy and hung, at Tap-pan, on Oc-to-ber 2. The fate of Ar-nold was worse than that of An-dré; for, though he saved his life, he lost all that makes life sweet and dear. He had

THE CAP-TURE OF AN-DRÉ.

no friends. Eng-lish and A-mer-i-cans shunned him as they would a snake. At the close of the war he went to Eng-land to live, and died there in the year 1804, at the age of 63.

Ar-nold was a bold, bad boy; and yet, in spite of this, he might have been a good man — for some-times boys out-grow their faults, and make up by great and good deeds for all the bad deeds they have done. But his heart was bad all the way through, and he did not love the truth, or fear God as he should have done.

You may not rise as high as a Wash-ing-ton or a Lin-coln, but it is your own fault if you sink so low as a Ben-e-dict Ar-nold, the great trait-or.

CHAPTER VII.

YORKTOWN: SEPT. AND OCT. 1781.

The year 1781 brought no ray of hope to the A-mer-i-cans; nor did the Brit-ish see their way clear to end the war. As you have been told, Gen-er-al Greene took the place of Gates, and had charge of the troops at the South. His whole force was but 2000 men, but in spite of this he sent Gen-er-al Mor-gan to the west of South Car-o-lina to put a stop to the wild deeds done there by the Brit-ish and their friends.

Corn-wal-lis sent Tarle-ton to push Mor-gan, and they met Jan-u-ary 17, 1781, at a place called the Cow-pens. The first fierce on-set of the foe made the

A-mer-i-cans yield; but Mor-gan soon brought them up, and in one grand charge on the Brit-ish lines they put the red-coats to flight.

As soon as this came to the ears of Lord Corn-wal-lis he made up his mind to take the field him-self, and was quite sure that he would win back all that had been lost, and bring to terms all the land that lay south of Vir-gin-ia. So he set out on a quick march to stop Mor-gan on his way back to Greene, and on Jan-u-ary 19 crossed the Ca-taw-ba Riv-er.

But Mor-gan was as shrewd as he was brave, and pushed on his troops at such a pace that they made out to reach Gow-an's Ford and cross the Ca-taw-ba two hours before the van-guard of the foe came in sight. It was quite dark when Corn-wal-lis reached the bank of the stream, where he made a halt till day-light. By this time a rain had set in that swelled the stream so that they would need boats to cross it, and these the A-mer-i-cans had tied up on the other shore.

As soon as the wa-ters went down Corn-wal-lis be-gan to ford the stream, and some of the A-mer-i-cans on guard at the ford were slain. Greene fled, and had just time to cross the Yad-kin when Corn-wal-lis came up; but as night had set in Corn-wal-lis thought he would give up the chase till the next day. Ere dawn the rain came down like a flood and the Yad-kin was full to the brim, so that the Brit-ish could not ford it.

The same thing took place when they came to the Dan Riv-er, and the A-mer-i-cans through-out the land could not but feel that God was with them, and kept them from the foe. And Corn-wal-lis gave up the chase.

As soon as Greene's troops had had a chance to rest, he led them back in-to North Car-o-li-na, crossed the Dan, and pushed on to Guil-ford Court-House, with-in ten miles of the Brit-ish camp. He reached there March 15, and drew his army up in three lines to wait the at-tack of Corn-wal-lis, who the same day came out to meet him.

Both sides fought with great skill for an hour and a half, when Greene gave the sign to his men to fall back, and both sides claim to have won the fight. Yet strange to say Corn-wal-lis turned back to Wil-ming-ton, while Greene kept on his march to the south, in hopes to drive the Brit-ish in com-mand of Lord Raw-don out of South Car-o-li-na. On his march, most of those who made up the bulk of Greene's corps left and went to their homes, and when he came near where the Brit-ish were, his force, though small, was for the most part made up of those who were pledged to fight as long as the war should last.

Greene wished to send word to Sum-ter, then on the San-tee, to get in front of the red-coats and check their flight. But there was no man in the whole ranks

WASH-ING-TON AT THE SIEGE OF YORK-TOWN.

brave enough to do this deed. It was a great risk. But a brave young girl, whose name was Em-i-ly Gei-ger, said that she would take the note to Sum-ter. Greene told her what was in it, so that in case there was need she might tear it up and tell Sum-ter what Greene wished him to know.

The girl got on a fleet horse, crossed the Wa-ter-ee at Cam-den, and while on her way through a dry swamp was brought to a stand-still by some Brit-ish scouts. They took her to a house at the edge of a swamp, and she was searched by a wo-man whom they hired. When left a-lone she ate up Greene's note piece by piece, and as naught was found on her to prove she was a spy or that she had come from Gen-er-al Greene, they let her go, and felt much shame at what they had done.

The girl went on to Sum-ter's camp, and soon he was on his way to help Greene, and check the red-coats.

Fights took place through the spring months in South Car-o-li-na and Geor-gia, in which there was great loss on both sides, and af-ter that of Eu-taw Springs the Brit-ish drew off their troops to Charles-ton and Sa-van-nah.

Late in A-pril Corn-wal-lis left Wil-ming-ton and marched north-ward to join his force with those at Pe-ters-burg. He tried to bring on a battle with La-fay-ette, who was then in com-mand of 3000 troops to guard the state of Vir-gin-ia; and as he failed in this he went to work with fire and sword to lay waste the land. He tried in the mean-time to seize the A-mer-i-can stores at Al-be-marle Court-House, but was foiled by the Mar-quis, who brought his troops be-tween his stores and the Brit-ish lines. For the skill he showed while in charge of the troops in Vir-gin-ia, the King of France made La-fay-ette Field Mar-shal of France, at the close of the war in A-mer-i-ca, which rank he held un-til his death in the year 1834.

CORN-WAL-LIS.

Corn-wal-lis soon went to Rich-mond, and from there to Ports-mouth, where La-fay-ette set out to meet him with a force of 4000 men. Wayne led the van-guard, and as he thought the Brit-ish had crossed the James Riv-er, he made a bold push for their rear. But lo! there they all were, and what was to be done must be done at once. So Wayne had his men fire, and then turn and run, and by this trick saved their lives. Corn-wal-lis did not think it worth while to give chase, and on Au-gust 1 crossed the James Riv-er and went to Ports-mouth. Not pleased with the place, he soon moved on to York-town, on the south side of the York Riv-er, and at once be-gan to build forts and to make it a strong-hold.

In July, 1781, Wash-ing-ton made his plans to move on New York and drive the Brit-ish from that town, and went in camp near Dobb's Fer-ry, where he staid for six weeks. He had sent out a call for troops, which were slow to come, and when Wash-ing-ton was told of the strength of the foe, and that a fresh lot of troops had been sent from Eng-land, he made up his mind to wait till the French fleet, in charge of Count de Grasse, came up from the West In-dies.

At length, in Au-gust, word came from Count de Grasse that he was a-bout to sail with his whole fleet and 3200 land troops for Ches-a-peake Bay. Wash-ing-ton at once set out for Vir-gin-ia with as large a force as could be spared from the posts on the Hud-son, and reached La-fay-ette at Wil-liams-burg on Sep-tem-ber 14.

In the mean-while the Count de Grasse with all his ships of war came in-to Ches-a-peake Bay, and on the way had a short fight with the Brit-ish Ad-mi-ral,

Graves, off the capes. More troops came by land to join the A-mer-i-cans, and all took up their line of march for York-town. On the last day of Sep-tem-ber they were all round the place, and the Brit-ish were hemmed in.

THE SUR-REN-DER OF CORN-WAL-LIS AT YORK-TOWN.

The A-mer-i-cans and French-men went to work the same night to build earth-works, and so still were they that the Brit-ish did not know they were near till the next day at dawn, and it gave them a shock to see the strong-holds they had built.

On Oc-to-ber 9 and 10, the A-mer-i-cans and French fired their guns, and with shells and hot shot raked the Eng-lish ships in the bay and did them much harm.

So fierce was the fire of the great field-guns that by Oc-to-ber 16 the walls of the Brit-ish earth-works were laid low and the guns thrown out of place. Wash-ing-ton said, "The work is done, and well done." Corn-wal-lis tried to get a-way by boats, but a fierce storm came up, the boats were swept from their course, and there was naught to do but to give up his sword. This was done, and on Oc-to-ber 19, the terms were signed, and the troops marched out and laid down their arms.

Not a cheer went up from A-mer-i-cans or French-men, for Wash-ing-ton had told them to check all sounds and signs of joy, and not add to the grief of the foe they had crushed.

The sur-ren-der of Corn-wal-lis sent a thrill of joy through the whole land. Bon-fires were lit; guns were fired, can-non roared, and all with heart and voice gave thanks to God that peace had come at last, and that A-mer-i-ca was free.

A horse-man was sent with all speed to bear the glad news to Phil-a-del-phia, where Con-gress then met. It was mid-night, Oc-to-ber 23, when he reached the town, and when the watch-men told the hour they cried out, "All's well! Corn-wal-lis is ta-ken!"

Men sprang from their beds, and rushed in-to the streets half dressed. The old State-house bell that had tolled for the first time on the Fourth of Ju-ly, 1776, now rang out in glad tones.

France shared in the joy, and A-mer-i-ca had proved her right to be the land of the free and the home of the brave.

CHAPTER VIII.

THE WAR OF 1812.

The war of 1812 is known as the sec-ond war for free-dom, and was brought a-bout in this way; For some time the Eng-lish had done much harm to A-mer-i-cans on the high seas. They had seized and burned their ships, and forced their sea-men to serve the King, and this was too much for the A-mer-i-cans to put up with.

The first fight took place at Fort Mack-i-naw, which was on a strait — or strip of land — be-tween Lakes Hu-ron and Mich-i-gan. This strait was two-score miles in length, and in the midst of it was a high rock, on which the French had built a strong-hold which fell into the hands of the Brit-ish in 1760.

The A-mer-i-cans gave the fort the name of Fort Holmes, and this was in charge of a small force of troops in the year 1812. As soon as it was made known that A-mer-i-ca and Eng-land were once more at war,

THE IM-PRESS-MENT OF A-MER-I-CAN SEA-MEN IN BOS-TON.

the Brit-ish troops in Can-a-da seized the fort at Mack-i-naw, and with the aid of the red men drove out the troops, and not a gun was fired.

As this was the key to the vast fur trade in the North-west, the A-mer-i-cans sought to win it back in the year 1814, but their force was too small, and they had to give it up.

By sea and land the Brit-ish and A-mer-i-cans fought, and brave deeds were done on both sides.

On Feb-ru-ary 24, 1813, Cap-tain Law-rence was in com-mand of the sloop-of-war *Hor-net*, which fell in with the Brit-ish brig *Pea-cock* off the coast of Bra-zil. Here a fight took place, and ere long the main-mast of the *Pea cock* fell, and she sank out of sight and took down with her nine Brit-ish and three A-mer-i-can sea-men.

CAP-TAIN BROKE.

While Law-rence was on his way home with the *Hor-net* and the pris-on-ers from the *Pea-cock*, the *Ches-a-peake*, Cap-tain Ev-ans, was out on a long cruise on the coast of South A-mer-i-ca. As she came in-to Bos-ton Bay a gale set in, her main-mast was blown away, and three of her men were drowned. The rest of the sea-men said that was a sign of bad luck, and they were loath to sail in her. Cap-tain Ev-ans was forced to leave her, as he had lost the sight of one of his eyes, and Law-rence, who had been raised in rank, was put in com-mand of her.

THE "CHES-A-PEAKE" AND THE "SHAN-NON."

At the close of May the Brit-ish ship-of-war *Shan-non*, Cap-tain Broke, with 52 guns, came up near Bos-ton and stood off for a fight. Broke wrote to Law-rence to meet the *Shan-non*, ship to ship. He said if the *Ches-a-peake* left Bos-ton it would be sure to be crushed by the Brit-ish force on the high seas, and it was as well for them to fight where there were no ships near to help or harm, and so test the for-tunes of the flags they bore.

Law-rence gave heed to this, and with Lieu-ten-ant Lud-low next in com-mand sailed out of Bos-ton Bay to meet the *Shan-non*, at noon of June 1, 1813. Near sun-set they were in the midst of the fight. When they had fought for twelve min-utes the *Ches-a-peake* saw a chance to take the wind out of the sails of her foe, to cross her bow, and rake her fore and aft; but just then a storm of shot and shell broke her spars and tore her sails so that the ship could not be moved. To add to this her top-sails caught in the fore-chains of the *Shan-non*, and held thus the decks of the *Ches-a-peake* were swept by the balls of her foe.

One of them struck the brave young com-man-der, and gave him his death-blow. As he was borne from the deck he said, "Tell the men to fire faster, and not to give up the ship; fight her till she sinks." The A-mer-i-cans made this their war-cry, and "Don't give up the ship!" nerved sea-men to be as brave as he who gave up his life for the cause, and whose death was such a great loss.

Broke's troops now swarmed the deck of the *Ches-a-peake*, and soon Lud-low met with his death-blow from a sword-thrust, and the *Shan-non* won the day.

Broke sailed at once for Hal-i-fax with his prize in tow, and the day be-fore he reached there (June 7) Law-rence breathed his last, wrapped in the flag of the *Ches-a-peake*.

Eng-land rang with shouts of joy, and the vic-tor, Cap-tain Broke won much praise, rich gifts, and high rank for the proud place he had won for the Brit-ish flag.

The A-mer-i-can war-ship *Con-sti-tu-tion*, 44 guns, had been on a long cruise to the coast of Spain, and was on her way back when the war of 1812 broke out. She set sail from An-nap-o-lis Ju-ly 12, for a cruise to the north, and at the end of three days fell in with the fleet in com-mand of Cap-tain Broke.

As she would stand no chance at all in a fight with such a force as she would have to meet, her cap-tain, Charles Stew-art, set to work to save her by flight. The sea was a dead calm, and there was scarce a breath of wind to stir the sails. Her boats were launched with strong sea-men to ply the oars. Guns were run fore and aft on the deck, and all the light sails that would draw were set.

Soon a breeze sprang up, and the *Con-sti-tu-tion* was well on her way when a shot at long range was fired from the *Shan-non*, but did no harm. When the wind died out the sea-men would pull at their oars, and when the breeze sprang up the sails did their work, and thus they moved on, but at a slow rate of speed.

The *Shan-non* made use of the same means and soon gained on the *Con-sti-tu-tion*, and the *Guer-ri-ere* (*geer-re-air*), 38 guns, joined in the chase, which was kept up all day and all night. At dawn of the next day the whole Brit-ish fleet were in sight, and bent on catch-ing the A-mer-i-can ship that showed such pluck. It was five a-gainst one, but the skilled sea-men kept such a space be-tween the *Con-sti-tu-tion* and her foes that not a gun was fired.

At sun-set of Ju-ly 19 a squall struck the *Con-sti-tu-tion*, and wind, light-ning, and rain raged on the sea for a short time. But she rode out the storm, and at sun-set was borne by a stiff breeze at the rate of 14 miles an hour, which soon took them out of reach of the foe.

At mid-night the Brit-ish fired two guns, and the next morn-ing gave up the chase, which had been kept up for more than two days.

Com-mo-dore Ol-i-ver Haz-ard Per-ry in 1812 had charge of the gun-boats near New York, and in 1813 was placed in com-mand of the fleet on Lake E-rie. He had to wait some time for troops, and had to go in-to the fight with less men than he had need of. On the e-ven-ing of Sep-tem-ber 9 he called his chief men round him and had a long talk with them. Ere they left he showed them a square blue flag on which, in large white let-ters, were the words,

DON'T GIVE UP THE SHIP.

When he should hoist this flag to the main-yard of his ship, the *Law-rence*, it was a sign that the fight was to take place at once.

The next day, Sep-tem-ber 10, the sun shone bright, and the man on the watch in the main-top of the *Law-rence* cried out, "Sail ho!" which meant that the Brit-ish fleet had hove in sight. In a short time Per-ry's nine ships were in range for the fight, and at the mast-head of the *Law-rence* was the blue flag that bore the words, "*Don't give up the ship.*"

The two fleets — like birds with wings out-spread — drew near each oth-er. The Brit-ish was in com-mand of Rob-ert Bar-clay, who had fought with Lord Nel-son in the East. His ships were named *De-troit, Queen Char-lotte, Lady Pre-vost, Hun-ter, Lit-tle Belt,* and *Chip-pe-wa.* The names of Per-ry's ships were *Law-rence, Ni-ag-a-ra, Cal-e-do-ni-a, A-ri-el, Scor-pi-on, Trippe, Ti-gress,* and *Por-cu-pine.*

The fight be-gan at noon, at long range, and the *Scor-pi-on* fired the first shot on the A-mer-i-can side. Fierce and more fierce grew the fight as the ships drew near each oth-er, and at times the smoke was so dense as to hide the scene from view.

For two long hours the *Law-rence* took part in the

OL-I-VER HAZ-ARD PER-RY.

fray   Her ropes hung loose, her sails were torn to shreds, her spars were bits of wood, and she was a wreck in-deed. The deck was strewn with blood. But one mast was in place, and from that streamed the

A-mer-i-can flag, which the brave Per-ry would not haul down in spite of his hard luck. All his ships but one had fought hard and done well, and that one was the sloop *Ni-ag-a-ra,* which kept out of harm's way.

She was a stanch ship, and Per-ry made up his mind to fly to her as she drew near the *Law-rence*, and to go on with the fight. He put on his u-ni-form, and took down the long flag that flew from the mast-head, and the square blue flag that bore the words "Don't give up the ship." Then he stepped in-to the small boat, with his broth-er, who was then but four-teen years of age, and with four stout men at the oars set out on his rash trip.

Those he had left on board the *Ni-ag-a-ra* watched him with fear in their hearts, as he stood up in the boat with the two flags wrapped round him.

The Brit-ish fleet brought all their guns to bear on the small boat, and a storm of shot and shell drenched the sea-men with spray and broke their oars, but not a man was hurt.

In a quar-ter of an hour Perry was safe on board the *Ni-ag-a-ra*, the flags he bore were hauled up to the mast-head and main-yard, and he dashed at once in-to the Brit-ish lines. In eight min-utes the flag-ship of the foe struck its col-ors, the fight was at an end, and the A-mer-i-cans had won the day. Per-ry sat down, put his cap on his knee, and wrote to Gen-er-al Har-ri-son, who had charge of the troops at Camp Sen-e-ca, a score of miles from Lake E-rie, in in these words, "We have met the en-e-my and they are ours — two ships, two brigs, one schoon-er, and one sloop.

The name of Per-ry stood high on the roll of fame, and A-mer-i-ca gave praise and thanks to her brave young he-ro.

CHAPTER IX.

LUNDY'S LANE: JULY 25, 1814.

At the close of the fight at Chip-pe-wa, July 5, 1814, the Brit-ish gen-er-al, Ri-all, fled down the edge of the Ni-ag-a-ra Riv-er to Queens-ton, put some of his troops at Fort George, and made his own stay near the lake, a score of miles to the west.

It was a great blow to the pride of Sir George Drum-mond, chief in com-mand of the Brit-ish troops, that his brave and well-drilled men should be put to flight by a lot of raw A-mer-i-cans. He made up his mind to wipe out the stain, and to drive the blue-coats out of Can-a-da. The A-mer-i-can troops were in com-mand of Gen-er-al Ja-cob Brown, who, as soon as he had cared for the dead and those who had met

WIN-FIELD SCOTT.

with wounds at Chip-pe-wa, gave chase to the Brit-ish, and laid plans to at-tack Fort George.

On July 24 word came to Brown that Drum-mond with 1000 troops, most of whom had fought with Lord Wel-ling-ton, had landed at Lew-is-ton. Their

PACK-EN-HAM LEAD-ING THE AT-TACK ON NEW OR-LEANS.

plan was, no doubt, to seize the A-mer-i-can stores — the guns, balls, and pow-der for use in war times — at Schlos-ser, a-bove the Falls.

Brown at once bade Gen-er-al Scott march a part of his force with all speed, and make a show as if he

THE FALLS OF NI-AG-A-RA.

meant to at-tack the forts at the mouth of the riv-er. At dusk of Ju-ly 24, 1814, as Scott and his troops drew near the edge of the Great Falls, he saw some Brit-ish of-fi-cers leave the house, mount their steeds, and ride off in haste.

Battle of Lundy's Lane.

He thought by this that the van-guard of the Brit-ish force was near, and made a dash in-to the woods to drive them out, when he was met by Ri-all, with more troops than he had had at Chip-pe-wa.

The A-mer-i-cans were in a great strait. They could not stand still; and if they fell back the whole A-mer-i-can force might be put to rout. So Scott made up his mind to stand and fight the foe — three times his strength.

At sun-set a fierce fight be-gan and did not stop un-til near mid-night. Ri-all's force, 18,000 strong, was on a rise of ground o-ver which went a road known as Lundy's Lane, the high-way to the west from the Ni-ag-a-ra Riv-er. On that height the Brit-ish had their large guns placed.

Scott found out that there was a blank space be-tween the Brit-ish and the bank of the stream, and he bade Ma-jor Jes-sup and the troops in his charge crawl through the brush-wood that grew in the space and turn the left flank.

This was done in the still, dark hours of the night, and Jes-sup and his men gained the rear of the Brit-ish, and kept back the troops sent up by Drum-mond. At the same time Scott fought Ri-all, and soon Brown came up with the main force to join in the fight.

Brown saw that there was no chance for the A-mer-i-cans so long as the Brit-ish had the earth-works on the hill. So he said to Col-o-nel Mil-ler, "Can you storm that work and take it?"

"I'll try," said Mil-ler; and he led his 300 men up the hill in the dark.

"Theirs but to do, or die." They kept close to a fence, where a thick hedge hid them from the view of the gun-ners and those who were on guard near them. When near the earth-works, Mil-ler and his men could see the gun-ners, with the fuse in a glow with which they were to touch off the guns at the word *Fire*.

Mil-ler chose his best marks-men, and told them to rest their guns on the fence, fix their eye on a Brit-ish gun-ner, and fire at the sign he would give.

Soon all the gun-ners fell dead at their posts, and Mil-ler and his men rushed in and seized the earth-works, and had a fierce hand-to-hand fight in the dark with the men who were to guard the guns and the gun-ners. The Brit-ish fell back, and though they tried they could not get back the earth-works nor the five large brass guns that were in it.

In the mean-time Scott fought hard and well, un-til he met with a wound in his arm. Gen-er-al Brown was hurt so that he had to be borne from the field, and Gen-er-al Rip-ley took his place. The A-mer-i-cans fell back to Chip-pe-wa, where Brown told them to take a brief rest and then come back, ere it was dawn, to take the field the Brit-ish had left.

But Rip-ley was slow to act, and the Brit-ish came up and took back the earth-work and four of the guns, and the field was theirs. Both sides claimed to have won the fight. The Brit-ish had 4500 troops, and

AN-DREW JACK-SON.

lost at least 878. The A-mer-i-cans had 2600, and lost 852. Mil-ler won much fame by his brave deed at Lun-dy's Lane, which was thought to out-shine all the bright deeds done through-out the war.

The war of 1812 was kept up for three years, and in that time 68 bat-tles were fought, North and South, by land and sea. A great fight took place at New

NEW OR-LEANS.

Or-leans, in which Gen-er-al An-drew Jack-son won great fame for him-self and for the A-mer-i-can cause.

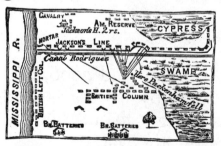

PLAN OF BAT-TLE OF NEW OR-LEANS.

He rose to high rank and was known by the name of "Old Hick-o-ry."

This brought the war to a close, and there was a long reign of peace in the land. Men laid down the sword and took up the plough-share, and the fields grew rich in corn and grain. Towns sprang up here and there on the plains where the red men used to dwell, and the Stars and Stripes waved at high-mast, and was all the more dear be-cause of the blood it cost to make it "the flag of the free."

CHAPTER X.

IN MEXICO.

A-mer-i-ca was a small child in 1815, but she soon be-gan to spread her-self and to add new States from time to time to the first 13, and to put more stars in her flag. The red men were not on good terms with the white men, for they drove them from the land to which they felt they had the first right. In 1832 the Sacs, Fox-es, and Sioux (*sooz*) set out to kill all the white folks who lived in the north-west. They were led by their chief, Black Hawk, and the war, which was soon brought to an end, is known as The Black Hawk War.

The red men in Flor-i-da were known as Sem-i-noles, and were good friends with the folks from Spain who laid claim to that part of A-mer-i-ca. They made raids on the States that were near, and did so much harm and shed so much blood that the U-ni-ted States made up its mind to drive the whole band to the wild lands west of the Mis-sis-sip-pi.

A SIOUX CHIEF.

This brought on what is known as the Sem-i-nole War, which be-gan in 1835 and was kept up for sev-en long years.

Tex-as was a part of Mex-i-co and und-er the flag of Spain, un-til the year 1845, when she be-came one of the U-ni-ted States. This brought on a war with Mex-i-co, and the first fight took place at Fort Brown on the third of May, 1846. Gen-er-al Zach-a-ry Tay-lor was chief in com-mand of the A-mer-i-can troops, and San-ta An-na of the Mex-i-cans.

Tay-lor crossed the Ri-o Grande, drove the Mex-i-can troops from the town of Mat-a-mo-ras (May 18),

OS-CE-O-LA.

and staid there till some time in Au-gust, when fresh troops were sent him. Gen-er-als Wool, Worth, and Scott were in league with Tay-lor, and did much to aid him, but their whole force was not half so great as the Mex-i-cans.

Gen-er-al Tay-lor was rough in speech, and did not think much of style. He rode side-ways on his horse more than half the time, and wore a slouch hat and an

SCENE ON THE COAST OF FLOR-I-DA.

old suit of clothes, and did not look at all like a great man. But he was much liked, and won for him-self great fame and the name of "Old Rough and Ready." If you will look at the list of Pres-i-dents of the U-ni-ted States you will find that he was the twelfth in line.

Gen-er-al Grant took part in the war with Mex-ico,

but he was then a young lieu-ten-ant. What he learned then was of great use to him, and well he proved the truth of the old say-ing that "a still tongue shows a wise head."

IN-DIAN WEAP-ONS.

A fierce fight took place Feb-ru-a-ry 23, 1847, at Bue-na Vis-ta, which was won by the A-mer-i-cans.

Grant saw a church close at hand, with a small bel-fry on top — a room in which a bell is hung. So he told the few men with him to take the field-gun a-part and bear it to the door of the church. Here they were met by a priest, who said they could not pass. But Grant told him that he might as well stand by, for they meant to come in, and the gun was set up in the tower, and sent its balls right in-to the Mex-i-can ranks.

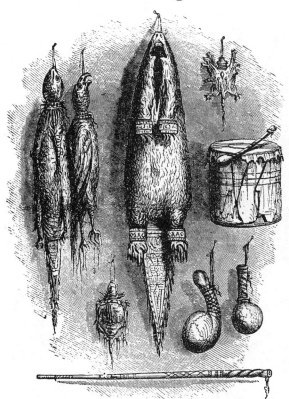

IN-DIAN OR-NA-MENTS.

It is as well to state that the Mex-i-cans had poor guns, and the A-mer-i-cans had no great fear of them. Their fields, too, were rank with a tall stiff grass, and when their balls went through it it would bend and sway like a wave of the sea. The A-mer-i-cans could tell by this just how to dodge the balls, and thus saved their lives, and made the poor Mex-i-cans feel that their foes bore a charm to save them from death, and to help them win their way.

In March the whole north of Mex-i-co was in the

hands of the A-mer-i-cans, and Gen-e-ral Win-field Scott was on his way, with 13,000 men, to Mex-i-co, its chief town.

They came down the Mis-sis-sip-pi on boats, and went on shore near Ve-ra Cruz.

CIT-Y OF MEX-I-CO.

Scott laid siege to this town on the 13th, and on the 27th it was in his hands, and the flag of Spain gave way to the Stars and Stripes. In the mean-time San-ta An-na came up with 12,000 men to meet the foe, and took post at Cer-ro Gor-do, a rough pass at the foot of the great hills known as the Cor-dil-ler-as. Here was a fort which was thought to be as strong as that of Ve-ra Cruz; but the troops in it soon laid down their arms, and the fort and all it held passed in-to the hands of the A-mer-i-cans.

ZACH-A-RY TAY-LOR.

On they went, these he-roes bold, and on May 15 came to Pu-eb-la, a large town, where they staid till the month of Au-gust to rest and gain strength, and to wait for fresh troops. Scott then pushed on, and was soon near the strong-hold on the out-skirts of the chief town, where King Mon-te-zu-ma once held sway and dwelt in grand state, and there was no lack of gold.

The camp at Con-tre-ras gave way to the A-mer-i-cans Au-gust 20, and the strong fort-ress of San An-to-ni-o struck her flag the same day. Scott's next move was to the heights of Chur-u-bus-co, and when this fell San-ta An-na fled in great haste to the chief town. The next day he sent out men to treat for peace with Gen-er-al Scott, who drew up the terms — which San-ta An-na signed. But this was a mere ruse, or trick, on San-ta An-na's part to gain time to add to the strength of the town; and when Scott found this out he set out on the war-path with fire in his eye. Less than 4000 A-mer-i-cans fought with 14,000 Mex-i-cans at Mo-li-no del Rey (the King's Mill) on Sep-tem-ber 8, and won the day, but with a loss of 800 men. The Mex-i-cans lost 1000 men.

This mill was long and low, as were all the houses in Mex-i-co, and there were rows of sand-bags on the roof, which made it quite a strong fort. Grant saw a chance to get up on the roof. An old cart stood near the mill; he brought it up, set it close by the wall with the thills up, and "chocked" the wheels so they would not roll back. Up this queer lad-der he and his men climbed to the top of the mill, drove out the Mex-i-cans, and held the fort.

The hill of Cha-pul-te-pec was doomed. On its top was a grand fort, built in fine style. This the A-mer-i-cans stormed with shot and shell Sep-tem-ber 12, and the next day the Stars and Stripes waved o'er its bro-ken walls.

That night San-ta An-na and his troops fled from the town, and the next day, at dawn, the folks there sent to Scott to beg him to spare the town and treat for peace. But he would make no terms; and on Sep-tem-ber 13, 1847, he marched in-to the town in great style.

San-ta An-na tried to get back what he had lost, but met with poor luck, and at the end of Oc-to-ber fled for his life to the shores of the Gulf, with the loss of one leg, which was shot off at the bat-tle of Bu-e-na Vis-ta.

CHAPTER XI.

WARS WITH THE INDIANS.

In all New Eng-land there was no tribe of red men quite so fierce and war-like as the Pe-quots. Their chief was named Sas-sa-cus. He was bold,

MAS-SA-CRE OF SET-TLERS.

cru-el, proud and fierce, and did his best to get the Nar-ra-gan-setts and Mo-he-gans to join him in a scheme to slay all the whites. But these two tribes were good friends of the white men, and had no wish to make war on them. So Sas-sa-cus made up his mind to do the task a-lone—that is, with his own tribe; and so great was his thirst for blood, that he slew all who came in his way.

JOHN EN-DI-COTT.

The chief fort of the Pe-quots was on a hill near the Mys-tic Riv-er in the town of Sto-ning-ton. It was not safe for a white man to pass up or down the stream with-out a guard.

The Eng-lish had a fort at Say-brook, which was some-what in a state of siege, as the troops did not dare to stir out for fear the Pe-quots would seize or slay them. In Au-gust, 1636, Cap-tain En-di-cott, of Sa-lem, was sent with 80 or 90 men to treat with them, and to make terms of peace with the Pe-quots, or to fight them for the wrongs they had done the white men. But the Pe-quots, as soon as they found out what the men had come for, ran off in-to the

PE-QUOT FORT.

woods and swamps, where it was no use to search for them.

In the spring of 1637, the Eng-lish made up their minds to make war on the Pe-quots. They were joined by the Mo-he-gans, with Un-cas at their head, and the whole force was in charge of Cap-tain John Ma-son. Some Nar-ra-gan-setts and Ni-an-tics lent them their aid, and while Sas-sa-cus dreamed of flight, his foes — 500 strong — were on the march to attack his strong-hold.

Soon they came to the foot of the hill on which the fort of Sas-sa-cus stood — with its three score and ten wig-wams shut in-side a strong log fence. Shouts and cries and wild war-songs were heard with-in the fort. At mid-night all was still.

Two hours be-fore the dawn of May 26, 1637, the troops set out for the fort. The red men, who had been in the van, now fell to the rear, and some of them were loath to fight Sas-sa-cus, for they looked on him as all but a god. But Un-cas was firm, and but for him the Nar-ra-gan-setts would have left the Eng-lish in the lurch.

As Ma-son drew near the door of the fort, he heard a dog bark, and one of the guards cry out, *O-wan-ux! O-wan-ux!* which is *Eng-lish-men! Eng-lish-men!* At once Ma-son fired on them through the logs, for the Pe-quots were in a dead sleep. Then the Eng-lish-men wheeled off, and fell on the main door, which was blocked up breast-high with brush-wood.

The Pe-quots rushed out, but the swords and balls drove them back to the fort, and they crept in-to their wig-wams. Then one of the white men took a torch and set fire to the straw that made the thatched roof of the wig-wams, and soon they were all in a light blaze.

The Pe-quots were wild with fear, and ran this way and that. Some of them climbed to the top of the high fence in their haste to get out, and some of them—at their wits' end—ran straight in-to the flames. But soon the smoke grew so dense that no one could breathe it and live, and in less than an hour there was naught left of the fort, and at least 600 Pe-quots were slain.

Sas-sa-cus was not there, but at a fort on the Thames, where Gro-ton now is. He sat still and grave when told what had been done on the Mys-tic, and his braves vowed to take his life if he did not lead them out a-gainst the pale face foes. Just then the blast of a trum-pet was heard. The white men were near, full 200 strong! The red men fled with their wo-men and chil-dren a-cross the Thames, through the dense woods and o-ver green fields to the west-ward, with the white men in full chase.

The Pe-quots hid in Sas-co Swamp, near Fair-field,

where, in a short time, all but Sas-sa-cus and a few who got off with him laid down their arms and swore

IN-DI-AN LIFE IN THEIR LOD-GES.

to live in peace with the Eng-lish. And this blow to the Pe-quots gave peace to New Eng-land for two-score years.

KING PHIL-IP'S WAR.

In the year 1621 Mas-sa-soit, King of the Wam-pa-no-ags, who laid claim to all the land from Cape Cod to Nar-ra-gan-sett Bay, came down to New Plym-outh with three-score of his men. They were all armed, and had on their war-paint, and were on their way to call on Miles Stand-ish, and to make terms with him for peace or war. Terms of peace were made, and Mas-sa-soit was a good friend to the white men as long

MAS-SA-SOIT AND THE PU-RI-TANS.

as he lived. He left two sons, one of whom was named Met-a-com-et, or Phil-ip. Phil-ip dwelt at Mount Hope, where he reigned o-ver the Po-ka-no-kets and the Wam-pa-no-ags, and for twelve years af-ter his fa-ther's death he kept the peace.

But when he saw how the white men spread them-selves o-ver the land, broke up the fields through

PIL-GRIMS ON THEIR WAY TO CHURCH.

which the red men had been wont to hunt the game, and drove them back from the shore so that they had no chance to catch fish, his heart grew hot with-in him, his young braves urged him to make war on the pale-face foes, and tried in all ways to make him hate them, and ere long he was forced to yield to them and to go on the war-path.

He struck the first blow at Swan-sey, Ju-ly 4, 1675, a place not quite four-score miles south-west of Ply-mouth. It was a fast day, and the white folks were on their way home from church when the red men fell on them and slew them.

The men of Bos-ton, horse and foot, joined the force at Ply-mouth, and all pressed on to Mount Hope, but found that Phil-ip and his braves had fled to a swamp at Po-cas-set. There they kept him in a state of siege for some days, but he at last found his way out and fled to the Nip-mucks, who were friends to his cause.

With 1500 braves Phil-ip set out to burn and slay till not a white man was left in New Eng-land. Men were struck down in the fields, their homes were set on fire, and death stared the white folks in the face at all hours of the day and night.

A score of Eng-lish-men were sent to treat with the Nip-mucks. They met near Brook-field in Au-gust, 1675, and the false red men slew the men from Bos-ton and set fire to the small town. Those who dwelt in Brook-field fled to one house in which they shut them-selves.

Night and day, for two days, the red men poured shot in up-on them, and thrust poles with fire-brands, and rags dipped in brim-stone, tied to the ends of them to fire the house. Then they took a cart and filled it with hemp and flax and set it on fire, and thrust this up close to the house by means of long poles. But as soon as it be-gan to blaze, a storm of rain set in and put out the fire, or else all in the house, three-score and ten souls, would have been burnt up in the flames.

In Sep-tem-ber, 1675, King Phil-ip and his men burned Deer-field, and slew some of those who made their homes there. The rest fled, and left a great store of wheat in stacks in the fields.

Cap-tain Loth-rop, with four-score young men, were sent from Had-ley to save this grain. As they drew near Deer-field, the red men sprang out up-on them, and but four of the brave white men were left to tell the tale. The fight was a fierce one, and in it 96 of the red men were slain.

In the year 1704 some French-men and In-di-ans came on snow-shoes from Can-a-da to Deer-field, to get a bell that hung on top of the small church in that place. It had been bought in France for a small church at Caugh-na-wa-ga, near Mon-tre-al; but the ship that bore it to A-mer-i-ca was seized by a New Eng-land man-of-war and ta-ken to Bos-ton. The bell was sold to the Deer-field church, of which John Wil-liams was the pas-tor.

The priest at Caugh-na-wa-ga coaxed the red men

to go with him and Ma-jor de Ron-ville to get the bell. When they came near Deer-field they found the snow four feet deep, with a hard crust on top that bore them well. On drifts that lay near the stock-ades, or strong-holds built of up-right logs like a fence, they crawled a-long in the gloom of night while all the folks in Deer-field were a-sleep. Ere day-light had set in, on March 1, 1704, their doors were burst in and the sound of the war-whoop roused them to a sense of their doom. Deer-field was set on fire. But one house and the church were saved from the flames. The bell was borne off, and found its place on top of the church at Caugh-na-wa-ga. More than two-score of the A-mer-i-cans were slain, and 120 were borne off to Can-a-da. Two of John Wil-liams' chil-dren were slain at his own door. With his wife and five chil-dren he took up his forced march to Can-a-da through the deep snow. His wife had a young babe in her arms, but two days old, and was in such a weak state that she fell down in a faint. The red man who had her in charge cleft her skull with his axe to rid him-self of the care of her. Her hus-band and chil-dren went on to Can-a-da, and for two years dwelt at Caugh-na-wa-ga with the In-di-ans, at the end of which time they were bought back and came to their own home.

But, one child, a girl of ten years, named Eu-nice,

the red men would not part with. She grew up with them, and had the same tastes and the same ways as their own squaws. Once she went to Deer-field to see her own folks, but all they could say would not make her change her mode of life or leave the church which she had joined.

Phil-ip, proud of what he had done, made up his mind to strike a blow at Hat-field, one of the chief towns near Spring-field. But the Eng-lish were in wait for him and drove him back with great loss. He then went to Rhode Isl-and, where he was joined by the Nar-ra-gan-setts. Their chief, Ca-non-chet, had sworn to stand by the white men, and 1,500 men of New Eng-land marched out to seize him. They found the red men with King Phil-ip in a fort in a swamp at South Kings-ton, with food to last them through the win-ter. On De-cem-ber 19 the Eng-lish stood in front of the fort, and in a few hours 500 wig-wams were in flames, guns were fired, and great was the loss of life on both sides. Ca-non-chet was slain, but Phil-ip fled and found a safe place with the Nip-mucks.

In the spring of 1676 he set out on the war-path once more, and laid waste whole towns, fields, and farms in Mas-sa-chu-setts. But ere long the red men fought a-mong them-selves, and some of the tribes left Phil-ip.

THE FRENCH ASK-ING AID FROM THE IN-DI-ANS.

Cap-tain Church, an Eng-lish-man of much fame, set out to find the red men and to put a stop to their cru-el deeds.

King Phil-ip was chased from place to place, and at last went to Mount Hope, sick at heart. In a few days he heard that his wife and son were in the hands of the Eng-lish. He was now crushed. "My heart breaks," he said. "It is time for me to die."

He was shot by an In-di-an—a false friend—and Cap-tain Church cut off his head and bore it on a pole in-to Ply-mouth.

So died the last King of the Wam-pa-no-ags; and his death and the end of King Phil-ip's war brought to a close the reign of the red men in New Eng-land.

BRAD-DOCK'S DEFEAT.

The French, who had made homes for them-selves in Can-a-da, sought to take up more land in the new world, and with the aid of the red men to so guard the O-hi-o River that the A-mer-i-cans would have no use of it.

Their plans were found out, and on A-pril 2, 1754, some troops were sent from the South to the head of the O-hi-o River. George Wash-ing-ton led the van; that is, he went out with those who were first in the field. He was then but 22 years of age.

Braddock's Defeat.

Mean-while Cap-tain Trent, and those who dealt with the red men west of the great range of hills, had formed a band and set out to build a fort at the forks of the O-hi-o where three streams meet, and where Pitts-burgh now stands. On A-pril 18 a band of

FORT DU-QUESNE.

French-men and red-skins made an at-tack on the fort, drove out Trent and his men, built up the fort to suit them-selves, and named it Fort Du-quesne (*kane*). News of this deed came to Wash-ing-ton while he was at Will's Creek, and he at once took up his march for a point less than two-score miles from the fort. There he learned that a strong force of French and red men were on their way to stop him, so he fell back to the Great Mead-ows, where he built a *stock-ade*, and called it Fort Ne-ces-si-ty. A *stock-ade* is a line of posts set in the earth as a fence, to shut in troops.

While he was at work on this fort, scouts sent word to Wash-ing-ton by a red man known as Half-King, who was on good terms with the A-mer-i-cans, that the French were quite near his camp.

Wash-ing-ton, at the head of two-score men, set off at nine o'clock of a dark night for the camp of Half-King. The rain poured down, and they did not reach the red men's home till sun-rise the next day, May 28, 1754. Half-King and his men joined Wash-ing-ton's troops, and when they found the foe in a lone place a-mong the rocks, they at once fired on them. A sharp fight took place. Ju-mon-ville, who led the French, and ten of his men were killed, while Wash-ing-ton lost but one man. This was the first blood shed in the French and In-di-an war.

Troops made haste to join Wash-ing-ton at Fort Ne-ces-si-ty, and he set out for Fort Du-quesne with 400 men. But when word came to him that a large force of red men and a few of the French were on

BRAD-DOCK'S FORCES SUR-PRISED BY AN AM-BUS-CADE.

the way to meet him, he fell back to Fort Ne-ces-si-ty, where a fight took place on the 3d of July. It was kept up for ten hours, at the end of which time Wash-ing-ton was forced to make terms of peace. The next day the troops marched out of the fort and went back to their homes.

In 1755 a plan was laid by the A-mer-i-cans and Brit-ish to wrest Fort Du-quesne from the hands of the French, and on June 10, a large force of troops, with Gen-er-al Brad-dock at their head, set out from Will's Creek.

Brad-dock was a Scotch-man, and had fought in more than one war on Brit-ish soil, and was quite set in his own way. Wash-ing-ton made bold to tell him that it would be well to spread his troops out and fight as the red men did, for they would hide be-hind a tree, a bush, or a rock, and pick out the men they meant to kill.

Brad-dock curled his lips with scorn, and said, "What! Can you teach a Brit-ish gen-er-al how to fight? My men are too brave to skulk be-hind trees!" So his troops marched on, and on Ju-ly 9, crossed the Mo-non-ga-he-la and moved in close ranks a-long the south bank of that stream. At noon they crossed to the south shore, and thought themselves quite safe from the foe, when all at once a storm of shot and clouds of ar-rows struck them on their front and flanks.

What Wash-ing-ton had in vain warned them of had come to pass.

The war-whoops and wild yells of the red men were new to the Brit-ish, and filled them with a strange sort of fear. Brad-dock took the front of the fight, and did all he could to keep his men at their posts, and for more than two hours the bat-tle raged.

Brad-dock had five hor-ses shot un-der him, and at last he too met with his death-wound. When Brad-dock fell the few of his troops that were left broke ranks and fled. When Wash-ing-ton, who was then forced to act as chief, saw that the day was lost, he called in the A-mer-i-can troops and bore Brad-dock from the field that he might die in peace. The foes did not give chase. The Brit-ish left their guns and their dead on the field. In three days Brad-dock was dead, and his grave was dug in the deep woods, where by torch-light his form was laid.

This fight which came to such a sad end is known as *Brad-dock's de-feat.*

In 1758 Gen-er-al John Forbes set out with a large force of troops to move on Fort Du-quesne. It was known that the force there was small, and that the fort could be ta-ken with ease. But the march was such a slow one that by No-vem-ber 8, they were still two-score and ten miles from the fort. This pace did not suit Wash-ing-ton, who was quick to move and to act, and it was thought best to give up the scheme.

Just then word was brought that there were but few troops in the fort, and Wash-ing-ton was at once sent to the front. When with-in a day's march of the fort they were seen by In-di-an scouts, who took word to the French that the foe were on them in great force. The French were in great fear, and set fire to the fort that night—No-vem-ber 24—and fled down the O-hi-o in boats by the light of the wide-spread flames.

The next day the Brit-ish flag was raised o-ver the spot where the strong-hold had been, and the name of the fort was changed to Fort Pitt. The small town that soon grew a-round it was called Pitts-burgh, and the name clings to it, though it is much more than a small town now-a-days.

TIP-PE-CA-NOE.

Te-cum-seh, or *Wild-cat*, was the name of a chief of one of the tribes of red men who lent their aid to the Brit-ish. He was brave and bold, and in the year 1811 sought to have all the tribes in the South join with those in the North-west, and slay all the white men, that the red men might have the land to them-selves.

In the year 1812 he was sent out by the Brit-ish to

urge the tribes to join them a-gainst the A-mer-i-cans. The Choc-taws and Chick-a-saws paid no heed to his words, but the Sem-i-noles and Creeks did. He told the Creeks to throw a-way the plough and the loom, and cease to till the soil, for such work was not fit for brave men.

Te-cum-seh took with him his brother, who was called *The Proph-et*. He was sharp and shrewd, and made the red men think that he had pow-er from God to work strange charms, to heal the sick, and to save from death. So great was his fame that men and wom-en would come a long way to see him, and to learn of him what was to come to pass. The Proph-et was not much to look at, for he had lost an eye in his youth,

TE-CUM-SEH.

and his love of drink and the low life he had led made him seem an old man when quite young in years. It is said that he fell down one day, and was thought to be dead, but when his friends bore him to the grave he raised his eyes and said, "Be not fear-ful; I have been in the Land of the Blest. Call the tribes that I may tell them what I have seen and heard." They came, and he told them such strange tales that they had great faith in him, and from that time forth he was known as *The Proph-et.* He told them he could make pump-kins as big as wig-wams spring out of the ground, and corn so large that one ear would feed 12 men!

He warned the Creeks that the A-mer-i-cans had come to drive them out of their land, and told them that their friends, the Brit-ish, had sent him from the Great Lakes to ask them to go on the war-path.

The Proph-et had been told by the Brit-ish when a com-et would be in sight, and he told the red men that they would see the arm of Te-cum-seh stretched out in the sky, and they would know by that sign when to be-gin the war. The red men looked on him with awe, for the fame of Te-cum-seh and the Proph-et had gone be-fore them.

But there was one big brave on whom all their arts failed. His name was Tus-ti-nug-gee Thluc-co. At length Te-cum-seh said, "Tus-ti-nug-gee Thluc-co, your blood is white. You have ta-ken my red-sticks and my talk, but you do not mean to fight. I know why. You do not be-lieve the Great Spir-it has sent me. You shall be-lieve it. I will leave here at once, and go to De-troit. When I get there I will stamp my foot on the ground and shake ev-e-ry house in Toock-a-batch-a."

Strange to say, at a-bout the time Te-cum-seh must have reached De-troit there was heard a deep roar un-der ground all through Al-a-ba-ma. The earth heaved so that the houses reeled and shook as if a-bout to fall.

The red-skins ran out in great fright, and cried out, "Te-cum-seh is at De-troit! Te-cum-seh is at De-troit! We feel the stamp of his foot!" It was the shock of an earth-quake that was felt all through the South in De-cem-ber, 1812. At the same time a com-et was seen in the sky, and the Creeks at once rose up in arms.

On the night be-fore the fight at Tip-pe-ca-noe, the Proph-et stood in the midst of his dupes — 700 red men — and told them that the time to crush the white men had come. He brought out what he made them think was a mag-ic bowl. In one hand he held a torch, in the other a string of beads. Each brave was to touch this charm as a safe-guard from death, and then to take an oath that he would kill the white men. When this was done the Proph-et waved his arms this way and that and said o-ver some strange words to add strength to the charm. Then he said, as he held up the string of beads to make them think of their oath, "The time has come; the white men are in your pow-er. They sleep now, and will nev-er a-wake. The Great Spir-it will give light to us, and will keep them in the dark. Their bul-lets shall not harm us, but not one of our ar-rows shall miss its mark."

Then they sang war-songs and had a great war-dance, and wrought them-selves up in-to such a wild state that they were like mad-men.

THE BUF-FA-LO DANCE.

Let us now take a glance at the white men. At that time Wil-liam Hen-ry Har-ri-son was Gov-ern-or of In-di-an-a, and as soon as it was known that Te-cum-seh had gone south to stir up the red men to war, there was a loud call for troops. Har-ri-son

Tippecanoe.

went up the Wa-bash as far as Ter-re Haute *(high ground)*, and near there built a strong-hold which was called Fort Har-ri-son.

He sent some chiefs to make terms with the Proph-

WIL-LIAM HEN-RY HAR-RI-SON.

et, who turned from them with scorn, for he was bent on war. So the troops pushed on, and on No-vem-ber 6, 1811, went in-to camp with-in three miles of the Proph-et's town. Har-ri-son placed his men in the form of a large square, and soon the whole camp was in a sound sleep. There had been a slight fall of rain, and the night was dark and damp.

The red men from the camp of the Proph-et crept through the long grass, and with wild yells fell up-on Har-ri-son's camp. Such was their faith in Te-cum-seh and the Proph-et that they had gone out like a wild mob with no one to lead them. A fierce fight took place, which was kept up till af-ter day-light, when the red men were put to flight by the troops on horse-back. They left two-score of their dead on the field. More than three-score of Har-ri-son's men were slain.

The horse-men rode to the Proph-et's town and found no one in it. So they set it on fire, and Har-ri-son fell back to Vin-cennes.

This fight gave him great fame, and he had charge of all the troops in the North-west in the war of 1812, and was in Con-gress for a long term of years. When the time came to choose a new Pres-i-dent, the choice fell on him, and songs in praise

Of Tip-pe-ca-noe
And Ty-ler too

rang through the land. He took his place March 4, 1841, and just one month from that time he died.

LIT-TLE BIG HORN.

Such was the growth of the U-ni-ted States that the red men were pushed to the far West and the North-west. At times force had to be used to get them to move from the land on which they had lived so long that they felt that they owned it.

These wars caused much blood-shed, and both white men and red men did deeds that seemed more like the work of fiends.

GEN-E-RAL CUS-TER.

The Mo-docs were first found on the south shore of Lake Kla-math, in Cal-i-for-ni-a. Their name means "foes." They drest in skins. In their wars they held cap-tives as slaves, and sold them when they had a good chance. They were in-deed foes to the white men, and had slain those who had sought to make homes for them-selves in the "land of gold."

A man named Ben Wright thought they should be paid back for these deeds. It may be that some of

A CROW CHIEF.

his folks had been killed by the Mo-docs. So in 1852 he made a feast, and sent for a band of Mo-docs to share in it. They came in good faith, when Wright and his friends fell on them and slew 41 of the 46 who were there. The Mo-docs could not for-give such a wrong as that, and war with them was kept up till the year 1864, when they made terms with the U-ni-ted States,

AN O-JIB-E-WAY CHIEF.

gave up their lands, and said they would go else-where.

The white men did not keep their word with them,

and this made the red men hot with wrath. A clan known as Cap-tain Jack's band were so full of fight that their own tribe found fault with them, and they were told to go back to the Kla-maths. This they would not do, and in the spring of 1872 troops were sent to drive them out of Or-e-gon. The whites were forced back with loss, and the Mo-docs fled to the La-va Beds — where a vol-ca-no had once been and burnt it-self out — and there they were safe from their foes for a while.

In June, 1873, Gen-er-al Whea-ton tried to drive the Mo-docs from their strong-hold, but could not get with-in three miles of them, af-ter the loss of not a few of his troops. Gen-er-al Gil-lem met with the same luck. In the mean-time the U-ni-ted States had formed a plan by which they thought to make peace with these Mo-docs. A band of wise men were sent out to treat with them. They met with the red men for a peace talk on A-pril 11, 1873, when the Mo-docs shot down Gen-er-al Can-by and Dr. Thom-as in cold blood. This foul deed was the cause of a long and fierce war with the Mo-docs, and at last Cap-tain Jack and his band were forced to come to terms. The chief and three of his head men were tried and hung at Fort Kla-math, Oc-to-ber 3, 1873.

In 1867 the Sioux (*soos*) had made terms by which they were to give up all their lands south of the Ni-o-bra-ra Riv-er in Ne-bras-ka, and go to a new place in Da-ko-ta called the Black Hills, by Jan-u-a-ry 1, 1876. In the mean time gold was found in the place set a-part for the Sioux, and hordes of white men from all parts of the world flocked to the Black Hills.

On the strength of this the Sioux made raids on all the land a-round, stole all they could lay hands on, set fire to the homes that had been put up, and slew all those who dared cross their path. Their chief was Sit-ting Bull, and he would not come in and live on the land set a-part for him and his band. They stole so much land from the Crows, who were more fond of peace than of war, that they asked for help from the white men. A large force of troops were sent out, with Gen-er-als Ter-ry and Crook at their head, to drive the Sioux back, and to take Sit-ting Bull by the horns, as it were.

The troops had been in camp for some time, and it was a sad hour for their wives when they set forth to meet the foe. Their march was from Mis-sou-ri to the Yel-low-stone Riv-er in Mon-ta-na.

Gen-er-al George A. Cus-ter — a brave man, who dared do all that man could do — was at the head of the 7th Cav-al-ry.

The Sioux were forced back to the Big Horn Moun-tains, and Cus-ter and Re-no were sent on to find out just where they were, and how large a force they had. The Sioux were found in camp on the left bank of the Lit-tle Horn Riv-er.

The red men keep out-posts and fires on each hill-top so that no one could reach their camps with-out be-ing seen. The In-di-an scouts who were with the troops made out as well as they could that Sit-ting Bull had with him at least 1000 men.

Cus-ter thought that he and his 300 men were a match for so small a force, and did not wait for troops to come up to aid him in case of need. But Sit-ting Bull was more shrewd, and had sent here and there for aid till his band had swelled to five times the size it was when it fled to Big Horn.

Had Cus-ter known this he would not have been so rash, but on June 25 he charged on the Sioux and was met by a force more than ten times the size of his own. No one knows just what took place, for Cus-ter and all his brave horse-men fell in the fight.

Fresh troops were sent to the front, and the Sioux were so hard pressed that they fled to Can-a-da, with Sit-ting Bull and Cra-zy Horse, and set up their camp on the north side of the Milk Riv-er.

CHAPTER XII.

BULL RUN. JULY 21, 1861.

We now come to a sad, sad time. The Good Book says that "a man's worst foes are those of his own house-hold," which means it is worse for those who live in the same house to fall out than it is for those who are not friends.

FORT SUM-TER AF-TER THE BOM-BARD-MENT.

Now the whole U-ni-ted States had been like one great house-hold for a long term of years. U-ni-ted means joined; held firm and fast. But as bad boys and girls—old and young—can up-set a home and rob it of all its joy and peace, so some of those who made up the U-ni-ted States and should have been its best friends, proved false, and with hearts full of hate broke the bond that made them One.

IN-TE-RI-OR OF FORT SUM-TER AF-TER THE BOM-BARD-MENT.

Then men took sides. Some were for the North, and some for the South, and there were hot words, and fierce looks, and a mur-mur in the air that told that a storm was close at hand. It broke in A-pril, 1861, when the South fired on Fort Sum-ter, just off the coast of South Car-o-li-na, and forced her to haul down her flag.

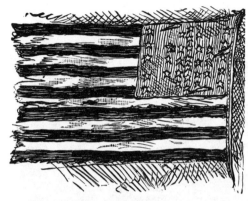

FLAG OF FORT SUM-TER AF-TER THE BOM-BARD-MENT.

An old man named Ruf-fin, who was three-score and ten years of age, fired the first shot, and made a great boast of this feat which caused such a flow of blood and tears. The shot from that gun sent a thrill of fear through the hearts of all true A-mer-i-cans, and the cry To arms! To arms! rang through-out the length and breadth of the land.

Troops from the North set out at once for Wash-ing-ton to guard that place, and the tramp! tramp! tramp! of armed men was heard on the streets of all the large towns. Most of the troops were "green" and had to be taught how to march and fight all at the same time; but they were full of pluck, and kept up heart in the face of the worst kind of ills.

The first hard fight took place at Bull Run, Ju-ly 21, 1861, be-

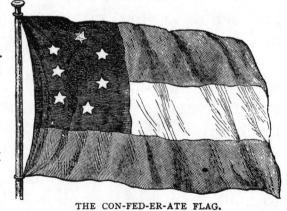

THE CON-FED-ER-ATE FLAG.

LIN-COLN RE-VIEW-ING THE TROOPS MARCH-ING THROUGH WASH-ING-TON.

THE SIXTH MAS-SA-CHU-SETTS REG-I-MENT IN BAL-TI-MORE.

tween Gen-er-al McDow-ell and his troops from the North, and Gen-er-al Beau-re-gard and his men, who had their post at Man-as-sas. Bull Run was a small stream in Vir-gin-ia that ran be-tween Man-as-sas and Cen-tre-ville.

The main road crossed the Run at Black-burn's ford, three miles from Cen-tre-ville, and on each side were two more roads that struck the Run at Un-ion Mills and the Stone Bridge. At all these points the South had guns and guards placed to keep back the foe. But McDow-ell found a good ford at Sud-ley Springs, two miles a-bove, to which there was no road, but which could be reached with ease through the woods.

IR-VIN McDOW-ELL.

His plan was to pass Sud-ley Springs with his right, and turn the left flank of the foe. The time to start was fixed for half past two o'clock of Sun-day morn-ing, Ju-ly 21, and at mid-night the troops were all a-stir. But it took them a long time to get out on the road, and the route through the woods was so long and so hard that the head of the line did not reach the stream till half past nine—three hours too late. Mean-while, Ty-ler had reached Stone Bridge on the turn-pike, and at half past six fired his gun, as he had been told to do by McDow-ell.

The noise of Ty-ler's guns roused the foe, and Col-o-nel Ev-ans, who was on the left of the Stone Bridge, made a change of front, and marched out to meet McDow-ell's men as they came out of the woods. These men were in charge of Gen-er-al Burn-side, and as soon as the head of the line came in sight Ev-ans fired on them, and for half an hour a brisk fight was kept up, by which time Burn-side had his troops in hand.

G. T. BEAU-RE-GARD.

Fresh troops and field-guns were sent to aid both, but the Un-ion troops had it all their own way, and soon put their foes to flight. Up the slope of land to its top-most crest rushed the troops of Col-o-nel Bee, and there found that a large force of troops held the heights, with Col-o-nel Jack-son at their head. Here

Bee brought his line in-to shape, and said to his men to rouse their hearts, "There stands Jack-son just like a stone-wall!" and the name of Stone-wall Jack-son clung to him from that day.

Johns-ton and Beau-re-gard came up to the aid of Bee and Bar-tow, and McDow-ell moved on them with 18,000 men. The Con-fed-er-ates now took their stand on a piece of high land at the base of which ran Bull Run and the small creeks that were a part of the stream. The main part of the hill was broad and bare, but at the south and east were thick pine woods, and on the west the Sud-ley road ran through a dense growth of stur-dy oak trees.

STONE BRIDGE.

In the first fight the Un-ion troops had seized the slopes that led up the hill from the turn-pike. A turn-pike road is one where toll-gates are set, and a tax is paid to keep the high-way in good order.

The Un-ion troops sought now to sweep the Con-fed-er-ates from the top of the hill, and the smooth space be-yond, and at noon they were in the midst of the fight.

Hard pressed, Ev-ans' line was a-bout to give way when Gen-er-al Bee came up with fresh troops, and gave it strength. Then the Un-ion line lost its hold, for the men were worn out with the long march and hard fight, and fresh troops were sent to their aid.

THOM-AS JON-A-THAN JACK-SON. (STONE-WALL.)

A charge made by some New York troops, led by Col-o-nel H. W. Slo-cum, broke the Con-fed-er-ate line, and the troops fled in wild haste to a field, where their flight was checked. By this time Jo-seph E. Johns-ton was on the field, to act as chief, and his gaze was fixed on the gaps in the hills through which he hoped to see fresh troops on their way to aid him. For well he knew that with-out these he could not hope to win the day. Two o'clock came — and no fresh troops were in sight.

On the Un-ion left Keyes' troops charged up the slope from the turn-pike, and found them-selves in a sharp fight with men on horse and on foot. But they reached the crest at last and seized the house there, which they held but for a short time. The great fight, mean-while, was on the Un-ion right, not far from the Hen-ry House, where the Con-fed-er-ates had placed their field-guns, and on which from a hill-top near the Un-ion can-non had played. Rick-etts' and Grif-fin's troops had charge of these guns, and with them were Ells-worth's Fire Zou-aves, drest like Turks in bright red suits with fez caps and white leg-gings.

JO-SEPH JOHNS-TON.

They made a great show, and were a rough lot of boys and men who could use their fists if their guns failed them. More troops from the East and West came up to swell the Un-ion force. The gun-ners and the Zou-aves were on the march, when all at once the Con-fed-er-ates fired on their flank, and Stu-art's

Black Horse Cav-al-ry came up in the rear, and the Zou-aves fell back. Then some Un-ion troops from Min-ne-so-ta were sent to fill up the gap, when down on them came a Con-fed-er-ate fire that thinned their ranks.

The loss was great on both sides.

It was now three o'clock. The day was hot, and the air full of smoke and dust. McDow-ell still felt that he could make the day his own. Johns-ton sighed for more troops. Just then he saw a cloud of dust on the line of the Man-as-sas Gap rail-way; and soon 4000 fresh troops swelled the Con-fed-er-ate ranks. Loud cheers and the rat-tle of guns were heard on the right flank and rear of the Un-ion troops, who fought their way up the ridge to the Hen-ry House.

PICK-ET DU-TY.

It was the van-guard of Con-fed-er-ate troops led by Gen-er-al Kir-by Smith. The Un-ion troops, worn out with their long march, faint from lack of food, and parched with thirst, gave way at the fierce on-set of the Con-fed-er-ates. Like wild-fire ran from

BAT-TLE OF BULL RUN.

man to man the cry that "Johns-ton's troops had come!" and they fled down the slopes, and ran in wild haste from the field of blood.

Crowds drove out to see the fight, as they would have done if a cir-cus had come in-to town, and the heights all round were gay with folks — great and small — who looked on and thought it a fine show.

But there was no fun in it when the Con-fed-er-ates gave chase to the Un-ion troops in their wild flight down the slopes. Pale with fright the crowd rushed pell-mell down the heights, blocked the roads with their teams, not a few of which were up-set, and ran this way and that in their wild haste to find a safe place.

AR-MY HUTS.

As good luck would have it, Johns-ton gave up the chase, and the folks found their way home in a calm-er frame of mind.

McDow-ell saw that all was lost. He did his best to check the flight of his "raw" troops, but it was no use. They were not used to war, and no doubt thought they had done the right thing. For

> "He who fights and runs a-way
> May live to fight an-oth-er day."

But they soon learned to **stand** fire, and did good

work in the war, the first shock of which gave them such a great scare, as well it might.

The news of the fight at Bull Run sent a thrill of joy through the whole South. The Con-fed-er-ates were sure now that their cause would win, and they were full of pride, and made haste to add to their stock of arms, ships, and such things as they had need of.

The North was cast down, and hearts that had beat high with hope were now deep in gloom. But this did not last long. "There is no such word as fail" to those who set out with a high aim, and theirs was to save the Un-ion. They saw now, as they had not done at first, that the war was to be a long one; and if they would win they must stand firm, put their trust in God, and fight with all the strength they had.

MON-U-MENT E-RECT-ED ON THE BAT-TLE-FIELD.

CHAPTER XIII..

FORT DONELSON: FEBRUARY 16, 1862.

The year 1862 found the North and South at war in the heart of the U-ni-ted States, through which runs the Ten-nes-see Riv-er. This stream joins the O-hi-o Riv-er, and on both were a long line of strong forts and earth-works.

At a bend of the riv-er, twelve miles from where it joins the Cum-ber-land, the Con-fed-er-ates built Fort Hen-ry on the right bank, and Fort Hie-man on the left—on a high hill.

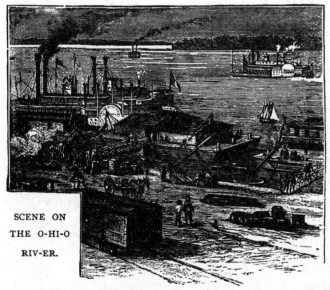

SCENE ON THE O-HI-O RIV-ER.

In Feb-ru-a-ry, 1862, a land force led by Gen-er-al U-lys-ses S. Grant, and a fleet of boats in charge of Com-mo-dore A. H. Foote were sent to seize those two forts.

Fort Hen-ry had 17 great guns, twelve of which

swept the riv-er, and there were less than 3000 troops in camp out-side. These were in com-mand of Gen-er-al Tilgh-man (*till-man*).

Foote brought four of his gun-boats in-to line, and

COM-MO-DORE FOOTE.

sent a storm of bomb-shells on to the fort. His fierce shots soon made them-selves felt. In a short time one of the large guns burst and killed three of the men at the piece. Then a shell came in and hurt some more of the gun-ners. It was not long ere one of the 42 pound-ers went off too soon and killed three men; and by this time the gun-ners lost heart, and ceased to work the small guns, which they felt were too light to harm the i-ron-clad gun-boats.

Tilgh-man did his best to urge the men on, but they were worn out, and in less than an hour the white flag was sent up as a sign that they gave up the fight.

AL-BERT SID-NEY JOHN-STON.

Word was at once sent by wire to the North: "Fort Hen-ry is ours! The flag of the Un-ion waves once more on the soil of Ten-nes-see!"

The troops out-side the fort fled to Fort Don-el-son, twelve miles off, and less than four-score men were left in the fort to lay down their arms to Com-mo-dore Foote.

Gen-er-al Grant and his land troops had found the roads deep with mire, and their march from the place where they went on shore was a slow one. They came up too late to take part in the fight, or to give chase to the Con-fed-er-ates, who thus had a good chance to get in-side the walls of Fort Don-el-son.

This part of the Con-fed-er-ate land force was then in com-mand of Al-bert Sid-ney Johns-ton. The

South knew that if Fort Don-el-son fell Nash-ville would be lost, so fresh troops were sent at once to add to its strength. On Feb-ru-a-ry 12, Gen-er-al Buck-

GEN-ER-AL GRANT.

ner brought a large force from Bow-ling Green, and the next day Gen-er-al Floyd came with more, and he took charge of the whole Con-fed-er-ate force.

Fort Don-el-son stood on the high left bank of the

Cum-ber-land Riv-er, two-score miles from where it pours it-self in-to the O-hi-o. It was a large field-work near the town of Do-ver, and on the land side of it there were hills and dales and deep sloughs that made it still more of a strong-hold.

JOHN A. McCLER-NAND.

At Fort Hen-ry Gen-er-al Grant placed his army in three parts, in charge of McCler-nand, Smith, and Lew Wal-lace. Foote went back to Cai-ro (*ki-ro*) to take his mor-tar boats—those that threw the bomb-shells—up the Cum-ber-land to aid in the fight.

On the morn-ing of Feb-ru-ary 12, 1862, McCler-nand and Smith set out for Fort Don-el-son, while Wal-lace stayed to hold the forts on the Ten-nes-see. That night Fort Don-el-son was hemmed in. On all sides were Un-ion troops. At dawn of the 13th the Un-ion guns were fired and a fierce fight took place, and Grant's men were forced back with great loss. The night grew cold, and a fierce rain-storm set in. Grant's men had no tents, and they were chilled through and through. They dared not light camp-fires, for fear of the guns of their foes, and they were scant of food and clothes.

The next day, the 14th, Foote came up with his

I-RON-CLAD GUN-BOAT.

gun-boats and brought food and fresh troops, that were hailed with cheers of joy by the boys in blue.

By three o'clock in the af-ter-noon Foote had his gun-boats in range, a mile and a half a-way, and sent up a fire from all the guns that could be brought to bear on the fort. The Con-fed-er-ates did not send back one shot till the boats came up with-in point-blank range. Then all the guns on the shore, twelve in all, sent forth their fire, and a fierce fight was kept up be-tween the fleet and the fort.

But the shot and shell of the ships spent their force on the sand-banks round the fort, and not a man was killed, while the Con-fed-er-ate guns made their shots tell on the fleet. The gun-boat which Foote was on, which was the flag-ship, was struck at least three-score times; one shot killed the man at the wheel, and the Com-mo-dore was hurt in the foot. One by one the boats fell back, and at the end of an hour and a half the fleet gave up the fight, with a loss of 54 of its men.

The South was full of joy, and at once sent the news to Rich-mond. But when the sun went down that night the troops in front of Fort Don-el-son were in a sad plight. The cold was so sharp that the men dared not lie down to sleep lest they should freeze to death. Grant did not know what it was best to do.

On the morn of the 15th, ere yet it was broad day, Foote sent for Grant to come and see him on board the flag-ship, as he was too much hurt to come him-self. Grant set out on horse-back, and was forced to go at a slow pace, as the roads were in such a bad state, much worse than if they had been a mass of mud. Grant had thought that if there was a land fight he would have to bring it on him-self, and laid his plans for a long siege. But when he came back from the flag-ship he was met by one of his staff, who, with a face white with fear, told him that the Con-fed-er-ates had come out in full force and put McCler-nand's troops to flight.

Grant was four or five miles north of the left of his line, which was three miles long. He rode as fast as he could, and saw no signs of rout till he came to the right of his line,

DOU-BLE TUR-RET I-RON-CLAD.

where McCler-nand's men had had to bear the brunt of the at-tack. He was told that the foe had come out with their knap-sacks on, as if they meant to stay out and fight as long as their food held out. But they fell back when fresh troops came up, and that made it clear to Grant's mind that some of the Con-fed-er-ates had tried to force their way out of the fort, and that it was time now to strike the blow. So he told Col-o-nel Web-ster to ride with him and call out to the men to come in-to line, for the Con-fed-er-ates meant to leave the fort if they could, and they must do their best to keep them back.

This brought each man to his place. It was noon, and Grant was on the field, and he bade McCler-nand take back the hill he had lost. This was soon done by the brave troops, and they camped on the new won field that cold win-ter night. Mean-while Gen-er-al Smith had struck the Con-fed-er-ates such hard blows on the right that when night came on they were shut in the trench-es — or ditch-es — and there was no way for them to get out.

Scouts who had been sent out to view the land brought back the real state of the case, and Floyd, Pil-low, and Buck-ner saw that the game was lost. There was but one thing for them to do, but who was to do it?

Pil-low said, "I will not sur-ren-der! I will die first!"

Floyd said, "Nor will I. It won't do. It won't do."

He had once held a high place in Wash-ing-ton, and had sworn to be true to the Un-ion and to the Stars and Stripes. He had been false to his oath, and if caught would have been tried and no doubt hung, for his crimes were great. So he had good cause for fear.

Buck-ner, who was a brave man, then said, "I will sur-ren-der, and share the fate of my men."

In the night two small steam-boats had come up the Cum-ber-land. Floyd seized them and fled up the stream with part of his troops, while Pil-low, with the aid of a skiff, sneaked off in the dark and made his way to his home in Ten-nes-see.

Buck-ner wrote a note to Grant, to ask him on what terms he would make peace, and sent it out with a flag of truce.

Grant wrote back that he would make no terms but a free and full sur-ren-der, and said, "I pro-pose to move at once up-on your works."

Buck-ner did not like the style of Grant's note, but was forced to yield to what he thought were harsh terms, and at dawn of the next day 10,000 men laid down their arms, and the Stars and Stripes flung out their folds o-ver the strong-hold on the Cum-ber-land.

On March 9, 1862, the great sea fight took place at Hamp-ton Roads be-tween the *Mon-i-tor* and the *Mer-ri-mac*, which you will have to read of else-where, as there is not space in this book to tell it as it ought to be told. The *Mon-i-tor* was a new kind of boat — "like a cheese-box on a raft" — and it won the day, and fought like a spit-fire.

CHAPTER XIV.

SHILOH: APRIL 6 AND 7, 1862.

On the west bank of the Ten-nes-see, near the south end of the State line, is Pitts-burg Land-ing, where steam-boats were wont to leave or call for freight on their way up or down the river. The banks at the Land-ing rise to a height of four-score feet, and are cleft here and there by great chasms, through one of which runs the main road to Cor-inth. Back of the bluff is a flat piece of land, cleared near the shore, but rough and with a growth of woods out from the stream.

On a ridge three miles out was Shi-loh Church, built of logs in a rude style. Near it two small streams —Snake Creek and Lick Creek, five miles a-part— wound their way to the Ten-nes-see and came out on each side of Pitts-burg Land-ing. This ridge was held by Sher-man, with a lot of raw troops who were yet to take part in their first fight. McCler-nand was on his left with the troops that had fought at Forts Hen-ry and Don-el-son. Next to him was Pren-tiss with more raw troops; Stu-art was on the far left, and Hurl-but in the rear. Gen-er-al C. F. Smith's men were on the right in charge of Gen-er-al W. H. L. Wal-lace, who had served in the Mex-i-can War. Smith was sick in bed in Sa-van-na, with-in sound of

Battle of Shiloh. 159

the Un-ion guns, and from that bed he did not rise again.

The foe were in force at Cor-inth, where two great rail-roads joined: one that led through Mem-phis to the East, and one that led south to all the cot-ton States.

On A-pril 2 Johns-ton moved on the Un-ion troops, and seized a guard of five or six men five miles out from Pitts-burg on the Cor-inth road. Sher-man gave chase at once, and drove the bold horse-men three miles from the point where the guards were seized.

WILL-IAM T. SHER-MAN.

Grant had to keep watch on all sides, and it had been his plan to spend the day at Pitts-burg and ride back to Sa-van-na at night-fall. But there was such a stir at the front from A-pril 3 that he did not leave Pitts-burg till quite late at night.

On the 4th he set out in great haste for the front, from whence came the sound of guns. The night was dark, and it rained hard. Now and then a fierce flash lit up the sky and made the scene more weird and strange. Grant had to trust to his horse to keep the road. He had not gone far when he met Wal-lace and McPher-son, who brought word that all was still at the front. On his way back to the boat the horse slipped and fell on Grant's leg, and for two or three days he had to go on crutch-es.

The Un-ion troops were stretched out in one long line from Lick Creek on the left to Snake Creek on the right, both of which streams were so high that the foe had to make their at-tack on the front. They came up with such a dash that the line of Un-ion tents soon fell in-to their hands. They tried hard to turn the right flank which Sher-man held, and to ward them off the Un-ion troops had to fall back from time to time and take posts near Pitts-burg Land-ing.

In one of these moves Pren-tiss and his troops did not fall back with the rest, and by this means he and 2000 of his men fell in-to the hands of the Con-fed-er-ate foe.

Though most of Sher-man's troops had their first taste of war at Shi-loh—and some of them had their guns placed in their hands on the way to the field—"they fought like brave men, long and well," and had great faith in their chief, "Te-cum-seh."

On the 6th Sher-man was shot twice, once in the

hand, and once in the shoul-der, when the ball cut his coat and made a slight wound. A third ball went through his hat, and more than one horse was shot from under him in this great fight. His loss would have been a sad one for his troops had he been forced to leave the field at Shi-loh. It was the plan of the Con-fed-er-ates to turn the Un-ion left, sweep a-long the bank, seize their base at the Land-ing, and then drive them down the stream. For a time they held their ground, but in the hot fire that was sent back a ball struck Gen-er-al Al-bert Sid-ney Johns-ton as he sat on his horse and gave him his death-wound.

DON CAR-LOS BU-ELL.

It was now three o'clock and the battle was at its height. Bragg drove Stu-art and Hurl-but to the Land-ing. Bragg cried out to his men, "For-ward! for-ward!" Beau-re-gard's or-der had been, "For-ward, boys, and drive them in-to the Ten-nes-see!" and there was the stream close at hand.

One more dash, and they were sure to win the day! At five o'clock the out-look for the Un-ion troops was a sad one. But hope was not lost with Grant and Sher-man there.

On the top of the bluff, and just south of the log-house at Pitts-burg Land-ing, Col-o-nel Web-ster, of Grant's staff, had placed a score or more of large siege guns. These guns faced the south, and were on the edge of a deep gorge.

The right of the line was now — at the close of Sun-day — near the bank of Snake Creek, not far from a bridge which had been built by the troops to join Crump's and Pitts-burg Land-ings.

Sher-man had some troops in a log-house to guard the bridge by which Lew. Wal-lace and his troops were to come from Crump's Land-ing. Through the night the foe tried to drive Sher-man from this post, but he held it till he gave it up of his own free will.

Then the foe sought to turn the left flank, but were swept back by the fire from the gun-boats *Ty-ler* and *Lex-ing-ton* and from the guns on top of the hill.

At dusk Bu-ell came up with fresh troops and formed the left wing, and when it was quite dark Lew. Wal-lace brought 5000 more, which were placed at the right. That night a fierce storm set in and drenched the Un-ion troops, who were with-out tents. Grant sat un-der a tree. The bruise on his leg gave

CHARGE OF THE FED-ER-ALS AT COR-INTH.

him such pain that he could get no rest. For a change he went back to the log-house down by the shore. All night men were brought in here to have their wounds dressed, or a leg or an arm cut off, and these sights made Grant haste with speed to the tree.

The next day, the 7th, the troops on both sides rose at dawn, tired, wet, and faint for want of food. The Con-fed-er-ates were in the Un-ion camps, from which Bu-ell and Wal-lace meant to rout them. No time was to be lost. Beau-re-gard met the on-set with a firm front, and soon the whole field was in the fight. Now the Blue would seem to gain, then the Gray; then there came a lull, and at one o'clock the fight went on more fierce than ev-er.

At half past one o'clock Beau-re-gard sent word to his men to with-draw from the field. The last point held by him was near the road that led from the Land-ing to Cor-inth. At three o'clock Grant drew near that point, and gave the command to his men, *Charge!* With loud cheers and a run they burst through the woods, and the foe broke ranks and fled. By four o'clock the last gun was fired, and the fight was at an end on the field of Shi-loh.

The Un-ion loss was 1754. These were killed on the field. Beau-re-gard is said to have lost 1728 men in the two days' fight.

CHAPTER XV.
ANTIETAM: SEPTEMBER 17, 1862.

In the Spring of 1862 Gen-er-al Rob-ert E. Lee was placed in com-mand of the Con-fed-er-ates, as Johns-ton had been hurt in the fight at Fair Oaks. George B. McClel-lan had charge of the Ar-my of the Po-to-mac, and Pope of the Ar-my of Vir-gin-ia, and both had met with Lee and been swept back from their posts. Hal-leck was now chief of the Un-ion troops, and in Ju-ly of this year Lin-coln sent out a call for 300,000 men to serve till the close of the war. And they came.

ROB-ERT ED-MUND LEE.

Lee made up his mind to cross the Po-to-mac, strike Bal-ti-more, and fall on Wash-ing-ton in the rear. On Sep-tem-ber 2, he sent a van-guard to Lees-burg, and at the end of five days the rest of his troops came up, crossed the Po-to-mac at the Point of Rocks, and went in camp not far from the town of Fred-e-rick.

Here Lee hung out his flag, and thought to add to his force, but in-stead of that not a few of his men ran off, so that he lost more than he gained.

When McClel-lan heard of Lee's move, he left Wash-ing-ton with 90,000 men, and went out to meet the great Con-fed-er-ate chief. But at sight of such a force Lee fell back, and the Un-ion men gave chase in two long lines. Burn-side led the right, by way of Tur-ner's Gap, and the left went by the way of Cramp-ton's Gap, which was near Har-per's Fer-ry.

GEORGE B. McCLEL-LAN.

The Con-fed-er-ates had no thought that the Un-ion men would keep up the chase as they did; but on the morn-ing of Sep-tem-ber 14, 1862, a strange sight met their gaze as they looked down from the heights. The vale was filled with Un-ion troops, who pushed their way up South Moun-tain and fought for each inch of ground. Long-street came to the aid of Hill, who fought for the South; and Hook-er's troops, with Rick-etts', Re-no's, and King's, lent strength to

GUARD-ING A BRIDGE O-VER THE PO-TO-MAC.

the Un-ion side. At dusk Hook-er turned the left flank of the foe. Re-no's men, who had gained a foot-hold on the crest, fought hard till dark. At sun-set Re-no was killed at the head of his troops, and died

HAR-PER'S FER-RY.

just ere the cheers went up that told the fight was won. In the night Lee drew back to a point near Har-per's Ferry, which was held by Un-ion troops, in com-mand of Col-o-nel D. H. Miles. The Con-fed-er-ates, led by Jack-son and Lee, swarmed on the heights all round the place. Miles was told by McClel-lan to hold on, but he paid no heed, and did not try to save the war-goods stored at that place.

On the 15th the Con-fed-er-ates sent such a storm of shot and shell on the fort, that Miles soon showed the white flag, and the post with all its troops and stores fell into the hands of the foe. There were 11,583 men; and the spoils were 73 great guns, 13,000 small arms, 200 wag-ons, and a large lot of tents and camp-goods.

Lee had no time to gloat o-ver his prize, for the next day he found that the Un-ion troops were on their way to cut his ar-my in two. So he

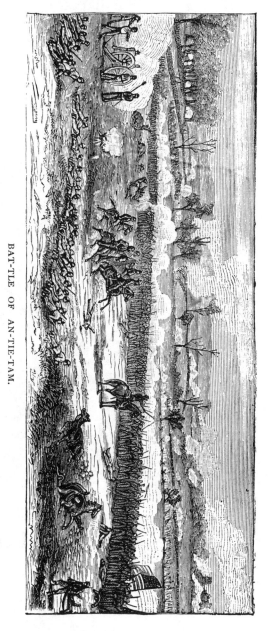

BAT-TLE OF AN-TIE-TAM.

with-drew his troops from South Moun-tain, and took his stand near Sharps-burg, while Jack-son by a swift march joined him on An-tie-tam Creek. Lee had 60,000 men, McClel-lan 87,000, well in hand.

AN-TIE-TAM BRIDGE.

On Sep-tem-ber 16, Lee's troops were on the heights near Sharps-burg, on the west side of An-tie-tam Creek, a small stream with few fords and four stone bridges. On the right of the Un-ion line were the corps of Hook-er and Sum-ner. In the fore-ground and near the An-tie-tam was Rich-ard-son's part of Sum-ner's corps. On a line with this was Sykes' part of Por-ter's corps. Down the stream was Burn-side's corps. In front of Sum-ner and Hook-er were long lines of field guns.

Let us now see how Lee's troops were placed. From the town of Sharps-burg two main roads led out. One ran east a-cross the creek to Boons-bor-o', and one ran north on the west side of the creek to Ha-gers-town. It was a mile from Sharps-burg to the stream.

A. E. BURN-SIDE.

Long-street was on the right and Hill on the left of the Boons-bor-o' road. Hood's part of Long-street's troops were on the left of Hill's line, and stretched out to the Ha-gers-town road. When Stone-wall Jack-son came up on the 16th he was placed to the left of the Ha-gers-town road, hard by a strip of woods.

It was McClel-lan's plan to cross the bridge on his right, strike the Con-fed-er-ate left with the corps of Hook-er and Mans-field, and if need be Sum-ner's and Frank-lin's, and if all went well to move Burn-side's corps on Lee's right, on the ridge that ran to the south and rear of Sharps-burg.

The first gun was fired by the Con-fed-er-ates at day-light of the 16th, but it was not till af-ter noon that Hook-er set out with a part of his corps to strike the Con-fed-er-ate left, where Stone-wall Jack-son was in com-mand. He drove them back from their strong-hold, and his troops slept on their arms that night on the ground they had won.

Mans-field's corps crossed the An-tie-tam late in the day, and at dawn of the 17th Hook-er went on with the fight. Both sides fought with all their might, but the guns on the east side of the creek drove the Con-fed-er-ates, with great loss, back of a line of woods.

Hood came up to Jack-son's aid, and the Con-fed-er-ates swarmed out of the works and fell on Meade, when Hook-er called on Doub-le-day for help. Fresh troops came up in the face of a storm of shot, and those who led them were the first struck down. A ball hit Gen-er-al Hook-er, and he had to be borne from the field.

The Un-ion men bore down on the Con-fed-er-ates more to the left, and were just about to win the day when fresh troops came up to aid the Con-fed-er-ates and drove them back in turn. This game was kept up for some time, till at last Gen-er-al Han-cock made a charge that drove the Con-fed-er-ates back in a wild flight. Then night set in and closed the scene.

The next day the Un-ion left, under Burn-side, fought hard for a bridge near Sharps-burg, which they had been told to hold. Here they were met by a sharp fire that more than once drove them back. But at noon fresh troops came up to Burn-side's aid and drove the Con-fed-er-ates back as far as Sharps-burg, then Hill bore down on Burn-side's left and drove them back to the bridge once more. Hill came up just in time to save Lee's

JO-SEPH HOOK-ER.

ar-my, for the Un-ion guns checked the Con-fed-er-ates on the east side of the creek, and they gave up the fight.

McClel-lan lost 12,460 men, 2010 of whom were slain on the field. It was thought that Lee's loss was more than this. The next day both sides were too worn out to fight; they had need of rest; and that night Lee and his troops stole a-way in the dark, crossed the Po-to-mac, and were for some weeks in camp at Win-ches-ter. McClel-lan failed to give chase, and as it was thought that more blood had been shed than there was need of — for the gain was not great — he lost his com-mand, and Burn-side took his place as Chief of the Ar-my of the Po-to-mac.

CHAPTER XVI.

VICKSBURG: MAY 19 TO JULY 4, 1863.

In the year 1862, the North and South fought, by land and by sea, 33 times, and still the war was not yet near its close. In 1863 the field of battle was in the south-west, and Gen-er-al Grant had charge of the Ar-my of the Ten-nes-see.

The South had blocked the Mis-sis-sip-pi River so that the North could have no use of it, and had great strong-holds at Vicks-burg and Port Hud-son.

Vicks-burg stood on a high bluff, one of the group of Wal-nut Hills, on the east bank of the Mis-sis-sip-pi, at a bold bend in the stream. The North had sent a fleet of gun-boats up the riv-er to take the fort, but

GUN-BOATS PASSING BEFORE VICKSBURG.

they failed to do so. All sorts of plans had been tried to bring on its down-fall, but still the flag of the South waved its folds on the Vicks-burg bluff.

Gen-er-al Grant had thought for some time that there was but one way to take the town of Vicks-burg, and that was to be-siege it. So he sent for Com-mo-dore Por-ter, and had a long talk with him, and the two laid their plans to place a ring of fire, as it were, a-round the town. Por-ter had a fleet of gun-boats at the mouth of the Ya-zoo Riv-er, north of Vicks-burg, and said that he would bring them and all the troops that were with him to the aid of Gen-er-al Grant.

COM-MO-DORE POR TER.

In the month of A-pril Grant sent a strong land force down the west side of the Mis-sis-sip-pi, and Por-ter ran by the guns at Vicks-burg, on the night of A-pril 16, 1863, with most of his fleet. On A-pril 27 he ran by the Con-fed-er-ate guns at Grand Gulf, so as to guard Grant's troops who crossed the stream at De Shroons.

Grant's son, Fred, a boy twelve years of age, was with him at this time, and on board one of the gun-boats a-sleep. His fa-ther left him there and hoped he would stay till Grand Gulf fell in-to their hands. But when Fred woke up, and found that his fa-ther had gone, he went out to search for him. He heard the sound of the guns on Thomp-son's Hill, and found his way to where his fa-ther was. He had no horse to ride on, and as there was no chance to cook meals, the boy had to look out for him-self, and get a-long the best way that he could.

GEN-ER-AL McPHER-SON.

Sher-man came down the west side of the Mis-sis-sip-pi to join Grant, McPher-son and McCler-nand brought up their troops and on May 8 the whole force pushed on and seized Jack-son, the chief town of Mis-sis-sip-pi. Then they turned to the west, and had a fierce fight at Cham-pi-on's Hill, in which they cut Johns-ton's and Pem-ber-ton's force in two, and put the foe to flight.

The Un-ion van-guard gave chase, and came up with them at the Big Black Riv-er, and one of the Gen-er-als led the charge in his shirt sleeves. The foe fled from the west bank, burnt the bridge, and left the men and the guns on the east side to fall in-to the hands of the North.

CAVES AT VICKS-BURG.

Then Grant swept on to the rear of Vicks-burg; Sherman took his stand at Haines Bluff, on one of the Wal-nut Hills, while McPher-son and McCler-nand filled out the line that was a score of miles in length, and stretched from the Ya-zoo to the Mis-sis-sip-pi.

Por-ter, with his fleet of gun-boats, lay in the Mis-sis-sip-pi, north of Vicks-burg, and by May 18, all the roads that led out of Vicks-burg were held by Un-ion troops.

For two weeks the Un-ion troops had been fed from the land through which they passed, but now they felt the want of bread. The cry of "Hard tack! Hard tack!" was heard all a-long the line; but in a few days, by dint of hard work the road was built through which could be brought all they had need of, and the cry was changed to cheers.

At two o'clock on the af-ter-noon of May 19, Grant gave the sign to storm the fort, and Sher-man's corps took the lead. McPher-son was at his left, on both sides of the Jack-son road, and McCler-nand at his left and as far out to War-

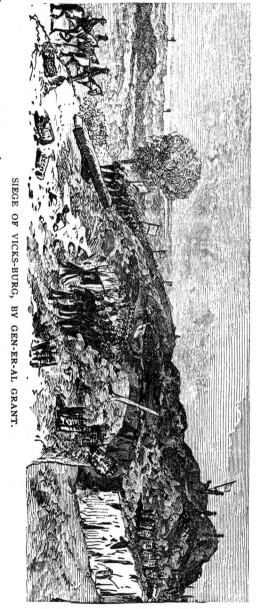

SIEGE OF VICKS-BURG, BY GEN-ER-AL GRANT.

ren-ton as his line would reach. There was a hard fight, and close work, but the Un-ion troops had to fall back.

Grant sent word to Por-ter to lend his aid, and all night of the 21st and 22d a storm of shot and shell poured in-to Vicks-burg. At ten o'clock the next day Grant's whole line moved on the works. At two points on the right they were swept back. McCler-nand on the left sent word that he held two forts. Then a charge was made by Sher-man's corps, and McPher-son brought his men up. But none of them could keep what they had won. Por-ter joined in the fray, but spent his shot for naught, and as soon as it was dark Grant drew off his troops, and then set in the siege of Vicks-burg.

The first thing to do was to build earth-works and to screen the marks-men from the guns of the foe. To do this sand-bags were placed on the tops of the walls, and a space left here and there as loop-holes for the guns. On top of these, logs were put, so that the men could walk at their ease when they had a chance to rest, and feel no fear that the Con-fed-er-ate marks-men would aim at their heads.

They had no mor-tars with them to throw bomb-shells, so they took logs of tough wood, bored them out for six or twelve pound shells, and bound them with strong i-ron bands. These were made use of and shells were thrown from them in-to the Con-fed-er-ate pits or trench-es.

The troops went to work with a will, and the black men who had come in-to the lines were hired to help

A RAIL-ROAD BAT-TER-Y.

them dig and build. Grant felt that now he had strength to meet the foe, and he drew his lines clo-ser and clo-ser round Vicks-burg.

On June 22 he heard that Johns-ton had crossed

the Big Black River to raise the siege and set Pember-ton free. This news put Grant in a great strait, as he was be-tween two fires.

At three points on the Jack-son road a mine was dug that led up to the Con-fed-er-ate earth-works, and on June 25 the mine was charged. The foe had dug on their side in hopes to strike the Un-ion mine, but failed to do so. At three o'clock in the af-ter-noon the fuse was lit and the mine blew up with a great noise. The top of the hill was blown off, and a hole left scarce wide e-nough for troops to march through.

A few of the Con-fed-er-ates were at work in the mines they had dug on their side to find and spoil those that the Boys in Blue had made, and these were thrown in the air, and some of them came down on the wrong side. One of these was a black man, who was more scared than hurt. Some one asked him how high he had gone up. "Dun-no, mas-sa," said he, "but I t'ink 'bout tree mile."

No good was done by these mines, and Grant made up his mind that no more should be dug.

In the mean-time, what sort of life did those lead who where shut up in Vicks-burg? The folks there had dug caves in the sand-hills on which the town stands, and here they spent their days and nights, and here some babes were born.

Food grew scarce, and when beef could not be had they ate mule meat, and were glad to get it. Their sole hope was that Johns-ton would come up from Jack-son with a large force and drive the Un-ion troops a-way.

But June wore on, and Grant drew in his lines clo-ser and clo-ser.

Johns-ton tried to help Pem-ber-ton, but could not, and Pem-ber-ton lost hope. For six weeks or more he had kept up a brave show, and had done all that he could to save the strong-hold from the clutch of Un-ion men. But it was no use. The end had come; and at ten o'clock on the morn of Ju-ly 3 white flags were seen on the Con-fed-er-ate works. The

GEN-ER-AL J. C. PEM-BER-TON.

sight of them sent a thrill of joy through all the lines.

Soon two men came up with a flag of truce and a note for Grant, which asked for a stay of blood-shed for a few hours, and a chance to make terms for the sur-ren-der of Vicks-burg. Grant sent back word that his terms were a full and free sur-ren-der of the town, its forts, and all the troops, and said that if Pem-ber-ton chose he would meet him in front of McPher-son's corps at three o'clock that af-ter-noon.

At three o'clock Pem-ber-ton with three of-fi-cers, and Grant with three of his staff, met on a hill-side near the Con-fed-er-ate lines. Pem-ber-ton did not like the terms Grant made at all, and left the place in quite a huff.

Grant made a slight change in his terms to please Pem-ber-ton, and sent the note to him at ten o'clock

IN-TER-VIEW BE-TWEEN GEN-ER-ALS GRANT AND PEM-BER-TON.

that night. This brought word from Pem-ber-ton that he would march out at ten o'clock a.m. on the Fourth of Ju-ly.

While the siege was kept up the Yan-kees had been heard to boast that they would dine in Vicks-burg on the Fourth of Ju-ly. Some-times the lines were so close that the "Yanks" and "John-nies"—as the

Con-fed-er-ates were called — could talk back and forth. John-ny would sing out, "Well, Yank, when are you coming to town?" and the Yank would say, "We'll dine there on Fourth of Ju-ly."

The news-pa-pers took this up and made great sport of it, but the boast came true, and the Fourth of Ju-ly, 1863, was a bright day for the North; for the sun shone on the Stars and Stripes, there were signs that the right would win, and that the long, sad war was near its close.

CHAPTER XVII.

GETTYSBURG: JULY 1 TO 4, 1863.

For some time the cry of the Un-ion troops had been "On to Rich-mond!" and Lee had kept a large force to guard the chief town on the "sa-cred soil." But in the Spring of 1863 he made up his mind to move on Phil-a-del-phi-a, and by the 8th of June Long-street's and Ew-ell's corps had joined Stu-art's horse-men at Cul-pep-er.

As soon as Gen-er-al Hook-er found out that Lee was on the march, and there were but few troops at Rich-mond, his plan was to move on that place and get at the rear of the Con-fed-er-ates. But to do this he would need to take troops from Wash-ing-ton, and as this was not thought to be a safe move nor a wise plan, Gen-er-al Hook-er was called from his high place, and on June 28 Gen-er-al George G. Meade was made chief of the Ar-my of the Po-to-mac.

Up to this time the State of Penn-syl-va-ni-a had sent out but few troops when the call was made for "300,-000 more," but now that the war was at her door she was up in arms.

When Lee saw this, and heard that the Un-ion troops were on his flank and rear, he gave up his scheme and bade his men fall back.

GEN-ER-AL STU-ART.

On the same day Stu-art's horse-men crossed the Po-to-mac and pushed on to Car-lisle, where they fell in with Kil-pat-rick and Cus-ter with their brave horse-men, and had a hard fight. They then kept at the rear of Ew-ell in his march to Get-tys-burg. Long-street was to cross the South Moun-tain range, and press on through Get-tys-burg to Bal-ti-more to keep Meade at bay.

Lee hoped to crush Meade, and then march on to Wash-ing-ton, or, in case he failed, to make it safe for him to fall back in-to Vir-gin-ia.

GEORGE G. MEADE.

Mean-while Meade brought up his troops in such a way as to force Lee to fight ere he could cross the Sus-que-han-na, and on the 29th he set out with Bu-ford and his horse-men at the left, Gregg at the right, and Kil-pat-rick in front.

He learned that night that Lee was on the way to Get-tys-burg, and he left for that place the next day, and his troops were spread out to the east and south of the town.

From Get-tys-burg good roads led to all large points be-tween the Sus-que-han-na and the Po-to-mac. West of the town and half a mile from it there is a high ridge on which stands the "Lu-ther-an Sem-i-na-ry." On this ridge there is a fine growth of trees its whole length, but at the north end, a mile and a half out, is a high knoll, called Oak Hill, which is quite bare on the south side. From this ridge the ground slopes to the west, and then swells up in-to a ridge on top of which is McPher-son's farm. West of McPher-son's ridge, a small stream—or run—flows in-to Marsh Creek. North of the town the land is flat and there is a clear out-look.

On the south is a ridge of bold high grounds, at the west end of which is Cem-e-ter-y Hill, and at the east Culp's Hill. Culp's Hill is steep on the east side, with a thick growth of woods, and at its base flows Rock Creek.

On the morn of July 1, Bu-ford, with 6000 horse-men met the van of Lee's army, led by Gen-er-al Heth, not far from Sem-i-na-ry Ridge, where a sharp fight took place. Rey-nolds, who led the left wing of Meade's troops, was on his way from Marsh Creek, with How-ard's corps at his rear, and Sick-les and Slo-cum with-in call.

The sound of fire-arms made him add speed to his pace, and he made haste to aid Bu-ford, who held the Con-fed-er-ates in check. Rey-nolds placed some of his troops on the Cham-bers-burg road; the Con-fed-er-ates fired, the Un-ion troops fired back, and then the fight at Get-tys-burg was be-gun.

Some of those in blue charged in-to a wood in the rear of the Sem-i-na-ry to fall on Hill's right, which was led by Gen-er-al Ar-cher. But they were forced back. Then more troops came up, led by Rey-nolds him-self, struck Ar-cher's flank, and seized him and a large force of his men. But when the charge was made, a shot from a Con-fed-er-ate marks-man struck Rey-nolds in the neck, and he fell dead on the field.

Gen-er-al Doub-le-day took his place, and at noon the whole of the First Corps was well placed on Sem-i-na-ry Ridge, and the rest of Hill's corps was close at hand.

WIN-FIELD SCOTT HAN-COCK.

Mean-while the van of Hill's corps took its stand on a ridge north of the town, and made threats on the line held by Gen-er-al Cut-ler. Doub-le-day sent aid to Cut-ler, and a sharp fight took place 'twixt the Blue and the Gray, and three North Car-o-li-na reg-i-ments were seized.

It was past noon when How-ard with his corps came on the field of strife, and took the chief com-mand of all the troops. To meet an attack from the north and west How-ard stretched out his lines to the length of three miles, with Culp's Hill on the right, Round Top on the left, and Cem-e-ter-y Hill in the cen-tre. At three o'clock in the af-ter-noon the Con-fed-er-ates, who were in great force, swept down on the Un-ion troops, and there was a fierce fight and great loss on both sides. The Blue line was forced back, and the day was lost.

Gen-er-al Meade was at Ta-ney-town — 13 miles a-way — when he heard of the death of Rey-nolds, and he at once bade Gen-er-al Han-cock leave his corps with Gib-bons and take the chief com-mand at Get-tys-burg. He came up just as the Blue line broke and was on a wild run for Cem-e-ter-y Hill. Sick-les and Slo-cum were there, and Han-cock told Meade that How-ard had his men well placed.

Then Han-cock went back to his own corps and took his stand a mile and a half in the rear of Cem-e-ter-y Hill.

Meade now brought his troops in a mass to Get-tys-burg, and roused them at one o'clock on the morn-ing of Ju-ly 2, when all but two corps were in line. Lee too brought up his troops as fast as he could, and took his stand on Sem-i-na-ry Ridge.

Thus the Blue and the Gray stood face to face for some hours, as if each one were loath to strike the

BAT-TLE OF GET-TYS-BURG.

first blow. Sick-les, on the left, 'twixt Cem-e-ter-y Hill and Round Top, had pushed his corps quite near the Con-fed-er-ate line, and Lee made an at-tack on him with Long-street's corps. There was a fierce fight, in which the Un-ion troops won.

While yet the strife was at its height, Gen-er-al Craw-ford, with six reg-i-ments of Penn-syl-va-ni a troops, swept down the north-west side of Round Top, and with loud shouts drove the Con-fed-er-ates through the woods to the Em-mits-burg road, and took 300 of them pris-on-ers.

Gen-er-al Humph-rey was then well to the front, with his right on the Em-mits-burg road, when Hill came up with a strong force, fell on him, and drove him back with a loss of half his men and three guns.

In this on-set Sick-les lost a leg, and Bir-ney took com-mand of the corps.

At sun-set Han-cock made a charge with fresh troops, drove back the Con-fed-er-ates, and took back four of the guns that had been lost by the Un-ion troops. The fight on the left came to an end at dusk.

Gen-er-al Slo-cum was chief on the right of the Blue line, and at the time Long-street made his at-tack on the left, Ew-ell had struck out on the right. It was a fierce fight. Up the north slopes of Cem-e-ter-y Hill the Con-fed-er-ates pressed, in the face of a red hot fire of shot and shell, close up to the mouths of the guns. Part of Ew-ell's corps tried to turn the Un-ion right by a charge on its weak part at Culp's Hill. But they failed, and the Con-fed-er-ates were held in check; but not till ten o'clock at night did the fight end, and then 40,000 men in Blue and Gray were left dead on the field.

Lee made up his mind to aim his chief blow at Han-cock's post on Cem-e-ter-y Hill, and at one o'clock on the af-ter-noon of July 3, 115 of his large guns poured their fire on this point. They were met by as fierce a fire from the Un-ion guns, and for two hours the earth a-round shook with a roar that could be heard for miles and miles.

GEORGE E. PICK-ETT.

Then the Con-fed-er-ate troops, in a line three miles long, swept a-cross the plain. Pick-ett led the van, and, 15,000 strong, made a wild charge up Cem-e-ter-y Hill. On they came with a rush! The can-nons had ceased to roar, and the roll of mus-kets was now heard! Shot and shell cut their way through the Con-fed-er-ate ranks.

Han-cock was struck with a ball and forced to yield his place to Gib-bons.

Pick-ett pushed on, while the troops of Hayes and Gib-bons poured a rain of shot in their midst. Part of the Con-fed-er-ate line gave way, and 2000 men and 15 flags fell in-to Un-ion hands.

Still Pick-ett moved on, scaled Cem-e-ter-y Hill, burst through Han-cock's line, drove back part of Webb's force, and raised the Con-fed-er-ate flag on a stone wall. But this was as far as he could go. Such a storm of shot rained down on Pick-ett's troops that they gave way at last, and soon 2500 men and twelve flags were in the hands of the Un-ion troops, and a host of the brave men in gray lay dead on the field. Wil-cox came up to Pick-ett's aid, but was swept back by the fire of the Ver-mont troops.

Mean-while Craw-ford came up on Lee's right flank from near Lit-tle Round Top. The Gray line broke and fled, and in this raid the whole ground lost by the Blue was won back, with 260 men, 7000 small arms, a can-non, and a lot of Un-ion men who had been left a whole day with none to care for their wounds. Thus, at near sun-set, Ju-ly 3, 1863, the fight at Get-tys-burg came to an end. That night and all the next day Lee's ar-my staid on Sem-i-na-ry Ridge, and on Sun-day morn-ing, Ju-ly 5, they were on their way back to Rich-mond.

Lee had said, when he went out, "I will whip them, or they will whip me;" and it was with a sad heart he left the field that he had hoped to win. His loss was not made known, but was thought to be at least 30,000.

Vicks-burg and Get-tys-burg were a great gain to the North, and worth all that they cost. It was felt that the war was near its close, and smiles of hope shone through the tears that filled the eyes of those who mourned their dead.

CHAPTER XVIII.

LOOKOUT MOUNTAIN: NOVEMBER 24, 1863.

In June, 1863, Gen-er-al Rose-crans was in command of the Ar-my of the Cum-ber-land, and had his post at Mur-frees-bor-o, Ten-nes-see, where he held the Con-fed-er-ate Gen-er-al Bragg in check.

The siege of Vicks-burg had drawn from Bragg's troops — who had gone to aid Johns-ton and Pem-ber-ton — and had Rose-crans moved at that time he would have been sure to win the day. But he did not move till late in June, when he drove Bragg south of the Ten-nes-see Riv-er and through and be-yond Chat-ta-noo-ga.

In the mean-time Bragg's troops came back to him, and with fresh strength he bore down on Rose-crans, so that he had to fall back in turn. He got his troops well in hand at Chick-a-mau-ga, some miles south-east of Chat-ta-noo-ga, and there the Blue and the Gray met on Sep-tem-ber 19.

Chat-ta-noo-ga is on the south bank of the Ten-nes-see, where that riv-er runs to the west. It is at the north end of a low strip of land five or six miles in width, through which runs Chat-ta-noo-ga Creek. To the east is a high hill, called Mis-sion-a-ry Ridge. On the west is Look-out Moun-tain, which at its north end is a steep cliff up to quite a height, then slopes off in-to farm lands.

W. S. ROSE-CRANS.

At Chick-a-mau-ga Creek Rose-crans drew up his men, 55,000 strong. He did not know that Bragg's force had been swelled by fresh troops till he had full 70,000, or he had been less bold. The Con-fed-er-ate right was in charge of Gen-er-al Polk, and the left by Gen-er-al Hood till Long-street should come.

Battle of Lookout Mountain.

Gen-er-al George H. Thom-as, who was on the left of the Un-ion line, by a move to seize some of the Con-fed-er-ates, brought on the fight at ten o'clock in the morning. It raged with fierce heat, and at first the Blue won; then the Gray would charge and drive them back, and so each side took its turn. Then there was a lull, but at five o'clock the Grays took a fresh start and pressed hard on the Blue line, when Ha-zen, who was in charge of what is called a "park"—which means a score of great guns—brought them to bear on the Con-fed-er-ates at short range, and the day was saved on the left.

BRAX-TON BRAGG.

Night closed the fight. The next day a dense fog set in, which gave Thom-as a chance to put up breastworks of logs, rails, and earth. The Con-fed-er-ates sought to turn the left flank, but Thom-as and his brave men stood like a wall in their way. A gap was in the Blue line, when Hood with Stew-art charged with great force, and struck so hard that the right wing gave way and fled to-ward Chat-ta-noo-ga. The tide bore with it the troops led by Rose-crans, Crit-ten-den, and McCook, but Thom-as and his corps stood their ground for some time. Gen-er-al Gran-ger came up with fresh troops, and then they formed a new line, fought their way to the top of a hill, turned their guns on the foe, and drove them down the south slope of the ridge with great loss. The Con-fed-er-ates fought hard, but soon the Un-ion troops held both the ridge and the gorge. But this state of things did not last long. The Con-fed-er-ates, led by Long-street, swarmed at the foot of the ridge on which stood Thom-as and a small part of the Ar-my of the Cum-ber-land. There seemed no hope for them, but Thom-as stood like a rock, and kept the Con-fed-er-ates at bay till the sun went down, when he drew off his troops to Ross-ville, for pow-der and shot were well nigh gone.

Gen-er-al Gar-field, Rose-crans' chief of staff, came up with word that Thom-as was to take charge of the whole Un-ion force, and that was the first that Thom-as knew of the fate of the right of the line.

Much blood was shed in this fight, and the loss was great on both sides, but the Con-fed-er-ates won the day.

On the night of the 20th the whole Un-ion force made its way to Chat-ta-noo-ga, while Bragg took his stand on Mis-sion-a-ry Ridge and Look-out Mountain. Bragg held all the roads near the place, and all the food for Rose-crans and his men had to be hauled three-score miles. Bread and meat were scarce, and their shoes and clothes well worn. They had burnt up all the wood they could lay hands on, and dug up the stumps of the trees. As there were no teams to draw the big logs, they made them in-to rafts and let them float down the stream to the south side, where they could be hauled on shore with poles, and borne by the men to their camps.

GEORGE H. THOM-AS.

In Oc-to-ber word was sent from Wash-ing-ton to Grant of the strait that Rose-crans was in, and the fear there was that he might fall back and let his whole force be seized by the Con-fed-er-ates.

Grant sent word to Thom-as by the wire that he must hold Chat-ta-noo-ga, and told him at the same time that he would be at the front as soon as he could get there.

Thom-as sent word back, "We will hold the town till we starve."

In a day or two Grant and his staff were at the front, Thom-as was made chief in place of Rose-crans, and the two went to work to get clothes and food for the men, and to bring up their strength so that they could stand the siege.

On No-vem-ber 4, Long-street set out with 20,000 troops, 5000 of whom were horse-men, to march on Burn-side, who was at Knox-ville. Sher-man was on his way to join Grant, who urged him to make haste.

Long-street had a rail-road as far as Lou-don, where he stayed for nine days. Sher-man reached Chat-to-noo-ga Oc-to-ber 14. The bad roads had made his march a slow one.

Grant's plan was for Sher-man to move on the right flank of the foe, cross the South Chick-a-mau-ga, and hold the rail-road in Bragg's rear. Hook-er was to do the same on the right, while Thom-as was to push his way from the cen-tre and strike the foe when most of them would be in the fights on the two flanks.

On the night of No-vem-ber 23, Sher-man set out to cross the Ten-nes-see at Brown's Fer-ry, and to place his troops back of the foot-hills, out of sight of the foe on Mis-sion-a-ry Ridge.

At two o'clock on the morn of No-vem-ber 24,

Giles A. Smith pushed out from the North Chick-a-mau-ga with 116 boats filled with 30 brave men well armed. These boats slipped down the stream with the tide and came to land near the mouth of the South Chick-a-mau-ga, when a rush was made on the guard known to be at that point. The men in gray were off guard and a score of them were seized. By noon the bridge of boats was built, and by half past three all the troops and the guns were on the south bank of the Ten-nes-see.

How-ard crossed at Cit-i-co Creek, to join Sher-man.

GEN-ER-AL LONG-STREET.

There had been a fine rain all day, and the clouds hung so low that the tops of the hills were lost to view. But ere long the foe turned their guns on Sher-man's men and did their best to drive them a-way. A ball struck Gen-er-al Giles A. Smith and he was borne from the field.

Hook-er was on the low ground at the west in front of Look-out Moun-tain, which was rough and steep and full of chasms on that side. He moved Gea-ry's men and some of Cruft's up Look-out Creek, where they were to cross. The rest of Cruft's troops were to seize the bridge, when Os-ter-haus was to move up and cross it.

The fog was so great that Gea-ry's move was not seen, and he pushed his way up the hill in the face of the guns on the top. The troops scaled the heights, cut their way through the trees that had been hewn down, drove the marks-men from their pits, and swept the Con-fed-er-ates up to the top of the ridge.

The fight in the clouds was a fierce one. In the af-ter-noon the foe were hard pushed and at last gave way and fled pell-mell down the steep chasms and slopes to the smooth plain at the base.

Grant and Thom-as were on a knoll, called Or-chard Knoll, where they were in full view of the fight, at least what could be seen of it.

The fog was so dense that it hid Hook-er's men from sight for a while. Then a cloud would lift and show where they were. But the roar of the big guns and the roll of the small ones could be heard all the time.

At four o'clock Hook-er sent word to Grant that

he could not be moved from his strong-hold; and Sher-man was well fixed at the end of Mis-sion-a-ry Ridge.

At mid-night all was still. Sher-man was to move on the foe at day-light the next day, and Hook-er was to move at the same hour.

The 25th was clear and bright, and the whole field was in full view from the top of Or-chard Knob.

Sher-man was out as soon as he could see, and by sun-rise had his troops to move on the main ridge, which was cut off from the point he had gained by a low pass, through which ran a road, and near which was a rail-road tun-nel.

The foe were strong at this point, and all their guns were brought to bear on Sher-man and his men. They were in great need of help, and Thom-as sent troops to their aid. Soon loud cheers were heard as Sher-i-dan and Wood charged up the ridge and put the foe to flight, and those in front of Sher-man like-wise took to their heels.

The foe had left Look-out Moun-tain on the night of the 24th, burned the bridge that spanned Chat-ta-noo-ga Creek, and cut up the roads as much as they could. It took Hook-er four hours to build the bridge and cross the creek, by which time the Con-fed-er-ates were a long way off. But Hook-er gave chase, and at Ross-ville came on a part of the foe which soon fell back, and were caught by Un-ion troops at the rear.

Chat-ta-noo-ga was now safe. Bragg had lost the strong-hold that was in his grasp, and which was of so much worth to the South. Burn-side was safe at Knox-ville, and had no fear of Long-street, and Grant had done the best that he could for the cause he held dear.

CHAPTER XIX..

THE WILDERNESS: MAY 5 AND 6, 1864.

At the dead of night on May 3, 1864, the Ar-my of the Po-to-mac, full 100,000 strong, set out on its march to Rich-mond. The men were strong, fresh, and full of hope. On the right were War-ren and Sedg-wick's corps; on the left Han-cock's. There were horse-men, and guns, and a long train of wag-ons — 4000 in all — and the roads were poor, and there were not a few streams to cross.

Burn-side's Ninth Corps had been left at War-ren-ton for a while, lest Lee should move on Wash-ing-ton, but by sun-down on May 5 all the Un-ion troops were on the south side of the Rap-i-dan. Then the

Battle of the Wilderness.

whole force pushed on to the great belt of woods known as the Wil-der-ness.

Lee was in force at Mine Run, and when he found out this move he marched out most all of his men to strike the flanks of the Un-ion troops on their march.

Hill and Long-street were to move to the right, by the Orange Plank Road. Ew-ell, who was near by, took his post that night four miles east of Mine Run.

RICH-ARD S. EW-ELL.

Grant bade Meade move his men on the morn-ing of the 5th. War-ren was to move to Par-ker's store, and Wil-son's horse-men to Craig's church. Sedg-wick closed in on War-ren's right, while Han-cock went to the south-west to join War-ren's left at Sha-dy Grove Church. At six o'clock War-ren sent word back that he saw the foe, and he was told to halt and get in shape to meet him. Wright, of Sedg-wick's corps, was sent to join on to War-ren's right, while Get-ty was to move by War-ren's rear and get on his left.

Soon the fight took place. Ew-ell was pushed back, but the Un-ion troops could do no more than hold their ground. Han-cock and Hill fought till night set in, and the gain was slight for Blue or Gray.

Grant was sure that Lee was near in full force, and had no mind to let him strike the first blow the next day. So he told Han-cock to move on the foe at five o'clock in the morn-ing. Wads-worth was to move at the same time and strike Hill's left; while Burn-side was to get in 'twixt War-ren and Wads-worth, and strike as soon as he had a chance to do so.

Lee brought up Long-street with 12,000 men to aid Hill, and the fight was a fierce one. It was kept up for an hour, at the end of which time the Con-fed-er-ates turned and fled like a wild mob, and ran for a mile and a half ere they came to a stop.

On the morn of the 6th, Sher-i-dan was sent to join with Han-cock's left and at-tack the Con-fed-er-ate horse-men who sought to get on the left and rear of the Un-ion troops. He met them at two points, and drove them back. The brave Gen-er-al Wads-worth met with his death-wound, and fell in-to the hands of the foe.

Long-street was shot and had to leave the field, and it was some weeks ere he could take charge of his troops. His loss was a great one to Lee, who had need of all his best men.

In the af-ter-noon Lee took the field him-self, and threw the whole corps of Long-street and Hill on Han-cock, who had a large force to aid him and a strong line of breast-works. Han-cock stood firm till the woods were set on fire by the shells, and the flames seized the logs and brush of the breast-works, and ran on the ground through the net-work of vines.

The wind blew the heat and smoke in-to the fa-ces of the men, and drove them from their posts, when the Con-fed-er-ates at once dashed in and placed their flags on the walls of the breast-works.

They were soon pushed out, and as night came on Lee fell back, and the Wil-der-ness fight was at an end.

The loss on both sides was great, and the gain was small, but for the hope it gave that the war was near its close, and the North would win at last.

CHAPTER XX.

ATLANTA: JULY 28, 1864.

In the first part of Ju-ly, 1864, Sher-man had forced Johns-ton to take his stand at At-lan-ta with his left on the Chat-ta-hoo-chee and his right on Peach Tree Creek.

Sher-man was then eight miles from the town. On the 17th Thom-as crossed the Chat-ta-hoo-chee close to Scho-field's right. McPher-son moved a-gainst the rail-way east of De-ca-tur, and the next day tore up four miles of the track. Scho-field seized De-ca-tur, and at the same time, on the 19th, Thom-as crossed Peach Tree Creek in the face of the Con-fed-er-ate earth-works, and fought his way step by step.

At this date Gen-er-al Rous-seau, who had swept through Al-a-bam-a and Geor-gia, joined Sher-man with 2000 horse-men, and on the 20th the Un-ion troops had all closed in and shaped their course to At-lan-ta. On the af-ter-noon of that day — at four o'clock — Hood set out from At-lan-ta and struck Hook-er's corps with great strength, but was forced back to his strong-holds, with a loss of at least 5000 men, 500 of whom were left dead on the field. Sher-man's loss was 1500.

The next morn, the 21st, the Con-fed-er-ates had left their post on the south side of Peach Tree Creek, and Sher-man thought they were about to leave At-lan-ta. So he pressed on to-ward the town, and at a point two miles from it was met by a strong line of earth-works, back of which swarmed a Con-fed-er-ate host.

The next day McPher-son moved from De-ca-tur to break this strong line, with Lo-gan's corps in the

SHERMAN'S GREAT MARCH THROUGH THE HEART OF THE SOUTH.

cen-tre, Dodg-e's on his right, and Blair's on his left. Hood left a force of troops in front of Sher-man to hold them, and by a night march to the flank and rear of the Un-ion troops struck them a sharp and not-looked-for blow.

At the same time Har-dee came up, and his men poured through a gap that had been made 'twixt Blair and Dodge. McPher-son had just called out to his men to fill that gap, when he was struck and killed by a marks-man shot. Lo-gan then took charge of the Ar-my of the Ten-nes-see, and the fierce war-fare raged for hours and hours. Late in the day there was a brief lull. Then a Con-fed-er-ate charge broke Lo-gan's line, and the troops fell back in wild haste, and let some of their large guns fall in the hands of the foe. Sher-man sent more troops to his aid, so that Lo-gan soon took back all that he had lost. The Con-fed-er-ates gave way, and fell back to their strong-holds. The loss on both sides was great.

Then raids were made by the Blue and the Gray,

GEN-ER-AL HOOD.

now on the right flank and now on the left, and for a whole week the fight was kept up, and much blood was shed.

Sher-man's long-range guns caused large fires in At-lan-ta, which was now in a state of siege. Hood drew off his troops, and on Sep-tem-ber 2, 1864, the Un-ion troops marched in-to At-lan-ta, and the Stars and Stripes flung out its folds o-ver the court-house.

A bold plan now formed it-self in the mind of Gen-er-al Sher-man. This was to march from At-lan-ta to the sea, tear up all the rail-roads, and cut off the Con-fed-er-ates from their grain fields and their war stores; in fact, to starve them out.

WILL-IAM J. HAR-DEE.

The rail-ways in and near At-lan-ta were first torn up. The wood-work was laid in piles, and a great bon-fire made of it, on which the rails were thrown. The heat would soon twist the rails out of shape so they could not be used at all, and no cars, of course, could come that way.

On the morn-ing of No-vem-ber 14, the whole of At-lan-ta was in flames, and while the fire raged, the bands played, and Sher-man and his men took up the line of march to the tune of "John Brown."

As soon as it was found out what Sher-man meant to do, the whole South was up in arms. Beau-re-gard was sent from the Ap-po-mat-tox to the Sa-van-nah to stop his march.

The cry all through the South was, "To arms! to arms! Burn what you can-not take a-way, and block up all roads on your route. Strike the foe in front, flank, and rear, by night and by day. Let him have no rest." Not a few lost faith in Jeff. Da-vis. They said it was "the rich man's war, and the poor man's fight," and they paid no heed to the rules laid down for them at Rich-mond.

Sher-man kept on his march, and his troops fed them-selves from the farms and fields through which they went. At Gris-wolds-ville there was a sharp fight, on No-vem-ber 22, with some of Har-dee's troops sent up from Sa-van-nah, but they were put to flight with a loss of 2500 men.

While at work on a bridge of boats, on the O-co-nee, Wheel-er came up with his horse-men and had a brush — that is, a short fight — with Kil-pat-rick, who drove them back.

On the 30th Sher-man's whole force had passed the

O-gee-chee, and as the chief rail-ways in Geor-gia were all torn up, the time had come for him to seize the State.

Then he set out for the sea, through swamps and sands, and though now and then he had a fight on the way, the Con-fed-er-ates were not seen in force till he was near Sa-van-nah. All the roads that led to that place — the chief town in the State — were blocked with earth-works, guns, and trees that had been cut down. These were turned, and by De-cem-ber 10 the Con-fed-er-ates were shut in Sa-van-nah, with the At-lan-tic on one side, and no way to get out by land.

But Fort Mc Al-lis-ter, at the mouth of the O-gee-chee, was a bar to Sher-man's march to the sea, where lay the Un-ion fleet. It was a strong fort, and had in it at least 200 men.

Gen-er-al Ha-zen was told to seize it, and on De-cem-ber 13 he crossed the O-gee-chee at King's Bridge, and at one o'clock was in front of the fort. Sher-man and How-ard went to a high place, and each, with a field-glass in hand, kept a close watch on all that was done at the front.

Ha-zen's bu-gles blew, and the men charged up the walls of the fort, and fought hand-to-hand with the foe, who sought to drive them back. But on and on went the bold men in Blue, and soon the fort and all it held were in their hands. As soon as Sher-man and How-ard saw the Stars and Stripes float from Fort McAl-lis-ter, they took a small boat for that point, and gave no thought to the bomb-shells and such things that were strewn on the bed of the stream.

Sher-man called on Har-dee to yield up his sword and to lay down his arms. But Har-dee would not, and on the dark night of De-cem-ber 20, when a fierce storm raged, he stole out of Sa-van-nah with 15,000 men and made his way to Charles-ton.

The Un-ion troops marched in-to Sa-van-nah De-cem-ber 22, 1864, and this was the end of Sher-man's March to the Sea, which won him great fame, and which has been told so well in prose and in song that old and young ought to know it by heart.

CHAPTER XXI.
WITH SHERIDAN.

At the close of the Wil-der-ness fight Sher-i-dan was sent out to tear up all the rail-roads that led in or out of Rich-mond, so that Lee and his force would be shut up in that town.

This was the first of the great raids which he led, and which are so linked with the name and fame of "Lit-tle Phil."

He pushed on with a dash, fought in the same way, and did so much good for the cause that he was placed at the head of a large force of troops. This was on Au-gust 7, and he took his stand at Har-per's Fer-ry, and at the end of a month had his troops well in hand.

The Con-fed-er-ate Ear-ly tried to lure him up the vale that he might flank him, but Sher-i-dan was too shrewd for him, and kept a close watch on the foe.

Grant went to see him, and to view the land. Sher-i-dan told him that he wished to move on the foe at once, and was sure he could whip them. Grant said, "Go in!" for he had great faith in Sher-i-dan, and knew that he would not fail in what he set out to do.

GEN-ER-AL SHER-I-DAN.

Then Sher-i-dan went out to meet Ear-ly, and the two lines met at O-pe-quan Creek, a few miles east of Win-ches-ter. Sher-i-dan kept a close watch, and when, on Sep-tem-ber 18, Ear-ly sent half his force to

TROOPS CROSS-ING THE SHEN-AN-DO-AH VAL-LEY.

Mar-tins-burg, Sher-i-dan at once put his force un-der arms, and at three o'clock the next morn set out for Win-ches-ter.

Here a fierce fight was fought, but at last Ear-ly was

put to flight, and Sher-i-dan chased him quite out of the Shen-an-do-ah Val-ley, and through the gaps of

SHER-I-DAN AT CE-DAR CREEK.

the Blue Ridge. Then he came back to Stras-burg, and took his stand on the north side of Ce-dar Creek.

In Oc-to-ber, a lot of fresh troops were sent to Ear-ly, and on the night of the 18th he crossed the hills and the north Fork of the Shen-an-do-ah. The next morn, in the dark, and, with a dense fog to hide him, he swept down on the left flank of the Un-ion troops, and seized the large guns that were to guard the whole line.

The Un-ion troops fell back in great fear, and with great loss.

At this time Sher-i-dan was at Win-ches-ter, at least a score of miles a-way, and as soon as he heard of the fight he set out at once for Stras-burg. He rode at break-neck speed, and came up with his men near New-town. They were like a wild mob, and were in haste to reach a safe place.

Sher-i-dan, with sword in hand, screamed out to them, "Turn back, boys! Turn back! We'll lick them yet!" and moved by the sound of his voice they turned back just in time to meet a fierce charge from the foe, and to drive them quite out of the Shen-an-do-ah Val-ley. Ear-ly's force was a great wreck; and with the few troops he had left he fled by night to Lynch-burg.

The fame of Sher-i-dan's great deed, known as Sher-i-dan's Ride, rang through the land, and won him much praise. The eyes of all the North were now on Phil. Sher-i-dan—the brave horse-man—who was yet to stand on the sun-crowned height, side by side with Grant and Sher-man.

Through the win-ter the roads were so bad that the troops could not march, or move their big guns, and they had to spend the most of their time in their camps. But this was not the case all through the South, for the war was still kept up.

Sher-man held Johns-ton in check, while Grant kept a close watch on Lee. In the spring of 1865 Grant feared, from signs that he saw, that Lee meant to slip out of Rich-mond some dark night, join Johns-ton, and strive to crush Sher-man. So he told his chiefs to keep a sharp look-out, and sent word to Sher-i-dan to join him at once, for there would be need of his horse-men.

It was the 26th of March when Sher-i-dan reached City Point. His men were worn out, and so were his steeds, not a few of whom had lost their shoes on the way. They had to be shod and put in good trim, and a few days of rest made them feel fresh and strong once more.

Grant told Sher-man that his plan was to seize Five Forks, drive the foe from Pe-ters-burg and Rich-mond, and end the war right there.

Sher-i-dan's face lit, and with a slap on his leg he said, "I am glad to hear it, and we can do it!"

All through the month of March there had been so much rain that the roads were not fit to use. But by the 29th, the ground had had a chance to dry and

Grant moved out with as much of his force as he dared take up the road to Five Forks.

But the rain set in once more, and in a short time the roads were in a bad state. Some-times a horse or mule would stand on what seemed to be firm ground. Then all at once one foot would sink, and as he tried to scratch his way out all his feet would sink, and he would have to be drawn by hand out of the quick-sands.

Sher-i-dan moved to Din-wid-die Court-House on the night of March 30, and took the road north-west to Five Forks. He had none but his horse-men with him, and on the way he fell in with some Con-fed-er-ate horse-men, and it went hard with him for a while. He at last drove them back; but when near Five Forks fell in with more troops and the same horse-men, and was forced to give way, and fell back to the Court-House.

Sher-i-dan sent word to Grant of the plight he was in, and War-ren's corps set out on the 31st to lend him aid. But War-ren was too slow to suit Sher-i-dan, who went out to meet him, and led the whole force him-self. He then pushed on to Five Forks. Ayres charged on the right, Mer-ritt on the front, and Grif-fin on the left with such force that they broke through a part of the Con-fed-er-ate line, and seized more than 1000 men. Mean-while Craw-ford came up and cut off the road by which they might have fled to Lee's lines, struck them in the rear, and seized four of their large guns.

Though hard pressed, the Con-fed-er-ates fought well and held their ground. But at last Sher-i-dan with all his horse-men charged o-ver the works with such a fierce dash that the Con-fed-er-ates threw down their arms, and fled pell-mell down the west-ward road. Sher-i-dan drove them till night closed in, and then he and Gen-er-al Miles camped on the ground they had won from the foe.

CHAPTER XXII.

PETERSBURG: APRIL 2, 1865.

JEF-FER-SON DA-VIS.

In June, 1864, Gen-er-al Grant made up his mind to move from Cold Har-bor, on the Chick-a-hom-i-ny, to some point on the south side of the James Riv-er. He and Sher-i-dan had had some hard fights with Lee's troops, the loss had been great and the gain small, and he felt it was not safe for them to stay where they were.

On the night of the 12th, part of the force set out

for White House, where they were to take boats at once for Cit-y Point. Some of the horse-men at Long Bridge crossed the stream on foot through the mud and drove off the men on guard there. A bridge of boats was then built, and the next day all of Grant's troops were on the south side of the James.

It was known that Lee had some gun-boats at Rich-mond, and these might run down at night and do much harm ere they could be sunk by the Un-ion fleet. So Gen-er-al But-ler, with wise fore-thought, had filled some boats with stones, and on the 13th, Grant sent word to have these boats sunk as high up the stream as the Un-ion troops could guard them, and keep them out of the hands of the foe.

BEN-JA-MIN F. BUT-LER.

On June 25, Burn-side be-gan to lay a mine to blow up the Con-fed-er-ate forts in front of him, and a-round Pe-ters-burg. He spoke to Grant and Meade of his

THE HOUSE WHERE GEN-ER-AL LEE SUR-REN-DERED.

scheme, and they thought it a good one, as it would give the men some work to do.

The mine was charged, and July 30 was the day set for it to be touched off. It was done, the fort, its guns, and 300 men were thrown high in air, and a great hole was left in the earth, full 100 feet in length, and from 20 to 30 feet in depth.

Then the great Un-ion guns poured their fire through the gap, but for some cause the scheme did not work well, and no good was gained by it. Grant lost 4000 of his men, most of whom were caught by the foe ere they could get back to their own lines.

In the spring of 1865, Lee was at Pe-ters-burg, and had built a strong line of earth-works there, where he meant to fight his last fight, and "hold the fort."

By A-pril 2, Grant had his troops well fixed in a long line that stretched from the Ap-po-mat-tox to the James.

That night a storm of bomb-shells was kept up in front of Pe-ters-burg, and the next morn, at day-break the Un-ion troops stormed its walls. Though checked now and then, they pushed their way through the Con-fed-er-ate lines, and drove the foe at all points.

On the same day the South-side Rail-way was struck at three points, and this was a great blow to Lee, who was now shut in-to the line of works close to Pe-ters-burg. Long-street went to his aid, and tried to win back some of the lost ground. But he could not do it, and at half past ten o'clock on Sun-day morn-ing — A-pril 2 — he sent word to Jeff. Da-vis that he could not hold Pe-ters-burg, and would have to leave it that day.

Da-vis was at church when the word came to him,

GEN-ER-AL LEE'S FARE-WELL TO HIS SOL-DIERS.

and it did not take him long to get out of Rich-mond. Lee moved to A-me-lia Court-House, and Grant set out to meet him. A few sharp fights were had on the way, but at last on the 9th Lee set up a white flag.

Grant and Lee met at the house of a Mr. McLean, at Ap-po-mat-tox Court-House. When Grant left his camp that morn he had no thought that Lee would give up the fight so soon. So he was with-out his

RU-INS OF RICH-MOND AF-TER THE WAR.

sword, and had on the loose blouse that he wore when on horse-back on the field.

When Grant reached the house he found Lee there. The two shook hands, and then took their seats. Lee had on a brand new un-i-form, with the bars and straps that told his rank, and at his side hung a fine

RICH-MOND, THE CON-FED-ER-ATE CAP-I-TAL, EN-TERED BY THE UN-ION AR-MY.

sword, the gift of the State of Vir-gin-ia. He was six feet high, and had a fine face and form, and was much thought of by his troops, and was, in fact, the hero of the South.

When he gave up the fight it was the death-blow to their cause, and the end of the four years' war that had cast its blight through the whole land.

Terms were made, and soon the dawn of peace set in, and men laid down their swords and guns, and went back to their homes and fire-sides, to their farms and trades.

I have not told you of all the fights that took place in the four years that the North and South were at war. The list is a long one—107 in all—some of which were on sea and some on shore, some on the coast and some in-land, so that the whole U-ni-ted States was stained with blood.

Love peace, hate strife, put your trust in God, and fear not:

> For He will help you in the fray
> And give you strength to win the day.

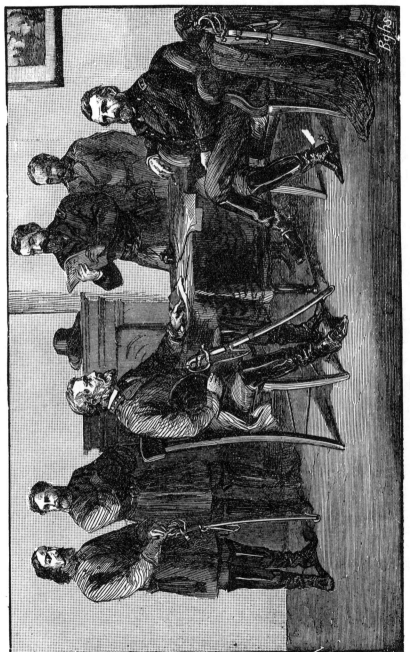

THE SUR-REN-DER OF GEN-ER-AL LEE.

CHAPTER XXIII.

THE WAR WITH SPAIN.

Cu-ba is an isle that lies near the coast of Flor-i-da. It was owned by Spain and ruled with a strong hand. All the good places in the land were filled by men sent from Spain, so the young men of Cu-ba had no chance to rise. They were taxed just as Spain chose to tax them. The Cu-bans felt that they ought to have some share of the places in their land and some voice in its laws. They want-ed to be free, and some of them rose and formed bands of men who vowed that they would have their rights. They raised troops, and took up arms and fought with the men from Spain. This made Spain all the more harsh with them, till the cru-el deeds done in Cu-ba roused the whole world. The U-ni-ted States felt that the Cu-bans were wronged, and they tried to help the poor folks, some of whom were half starved. They sent ship-loads of food to them, which did not please the Span-ish. They tried to keep back the food, and there were street fights in Ha-van-a.

Then the U-ni-ted States sent a ship of war, called the *Maine*, down there to take care of the rights of A-mer-i-cans. On the 25th of Feb-ru-a-ry, at ten o'clock at night, all the fore-part of the *Maine* was blown up. Two of the ship's head men and 264 of her crew were killed. Some were pinned down by bits of wreck or drowned like rats as the hull sank in the waves.

A great wave of grief and rage swept through the length and breadth of the land. The thought of

U. S. S. MAINE.

those poor men sent from sleep to their death fired each heart, and a cry of "Re-mem-ber the *Maine*" rang out on all sides. If the Span-ish had done this base deed, it was felt that they should pay for it, and it would cost them dear. So men were sent to look at the wreck, and they were sure from what they saw that the work had been done by foes.

So the mass of folk, touched by the woes of Cu-ba and roused by this great blow, made up their minds to help her to be free.

So they sent word to Spain that she must take her troops out of Cu-ba, and that they must all be gone by noon, on the 23d of A-pril. Of course, Spain did not wish to give up Cu-ba, and to keep it she went to war. The Pres-i-dent sent out a call for

BAT-TLE OF MA-NI-LA.
By permission of Truth Publishing Co.

troops, and they came in throngs from all parts of the land. Camps were laid out, and the men drilled each day and tried to learn the art of war. In May a great piece of news came to cheer the A-mer-i-cans. It was that the Span-ish fleet which lay in Ma-ni-la Bay had been taken by Com-mo-dore Dew-ey. Dew-ey had sailed from Hong Kong with his fleet, and he went to look for the Span-ish ships which he

AD-MI-RAL DEW-EY.

thought were near the Phil-ip-pines. He sailed by the fort in the night, and he pushed on, though two mines blew up right in his way. So he got close to the shore, where he could pour out a hot fire on the ships of Spain. He wrecked each ship till it could be of no more use in the war. Not one life was lost on the side of the A-mer-i-cans and not one ship.

Com-mo-dore Dew-ey showed in this work that he was a brave man and had a cool head. The Pres-i-dent raised him at once in rank and made him an Ad-mi-ral. In May the Pres-i-dent called for more troops. Com-mo-dore Schley sent word that he thought the Span-ish fleet which had played hide and seek so long was in the bay at San-ti-a-go. Some thought that the Span-ish Ad-mi-ral, Cer-ve-ra, knew too much to be caught in such a trap, but there they were. The next move was to fix things so he could not get out with his ships. Ad-mi-ral Sampson called on Lieu-ten-ant Rich-ard Hob-son to know what he thought would be a good plan. He said that if a ship was sunk at just the right point in the bay, it would keep the Span-ish fleet fast and sure. So they chose the *Mer-ri-mac* as the ship to be sunk, and Hob-son begged that they would trust the job to him. Sev-en men were found to go with him and risk the loss of their lives for their land. In the *Mer-ri-mac* were four score pounds of pow-der to wreck the ship. The men wore tights so they could jump in the bay and swim off; but Lieu-ten-ant Hob-son was in the same clothes he wore each day. There was a life-boat slung on one side, in which they might drop if they could. It was a great risk. If they did not jump in time, they would be blown up. You may think what brave men it took for such work. Those who watched the *Mer-ri-mac* saw her swing out in the bay, and they heard five of the charges go off. Then came a fierce fire from the ships of Spain that hid all the rest from view.

LIEU-TEN-ANT HOB-SON.

A boat start-ed out to search for the crew, and all the guns on sea and shore were trained on it. Still they kept up the search, though they did not hear a cry for help or see a sign of the brave men whom they feared had gone to their death. Where they looked they could see a sheet of flame, but just where Hob-son had said he would sink the ship could be seen the top of the *Mer-ri-mac's* masts. He had kept his word.

With sad hearts the men went back from their search, but they still had some hope that Hob-son and his brave crew were not lost. In a few hours came a flag of truce from the Span-ish Ad-mi-ral, Cer-ve-ra, which said that all the men were in the hands of the Span-iards, and as they had shown that they were such brave men, he would change them for Span-iards who might be in the hands of the A-mer-i-cans. The Pres-i-dent raised Lieu-ten-ant Hob-son ten steps in rank for this brave deed, and the men who were with him had a raise too.

Hob-son was kept in Mor-ro Cas-tle, and was not freed till near the end of the war. On June 10th the first A-mer-i-can troops landed in Cu-ba, on the shore of a bay called Guan-ta-na-mo. The foe shot at them from the woods, and some were killed, but the A-mer-i-cans shelled the woods and drove them back with loss. The first day's march of the A-mer-i-can troops on the way to San-ti-a-go ended in a fight. At a point near Se-vil-la some troops ran in-to a place where the foe had hid in great force. A hot fire met them, and some of their men were killed

ENTRANCE TO SAN-TI-A-GO DE CU-BA'S MOR-RO CAS-TLE.
From Scientific American.

or wound-ed. But they pushed on and drove the foe out of their trench-es. Colo-nel Roose-velt with his troop, who were called the Rough Ri-ders, was in the thick of the fight. He led his men and cheered them on, and did not seem to mind the balls that rained on him. The fight last-ed four hours.

GEN-ER-AL SHAF-TER.

On Fri-day, Ju-ly 1st, a great fight took place. A large force of Gen-er-al Shaf-ter's men with some Cu-ban troops met the Span-ish on the east side of San-ti-a-go. The Span-ish had earth-works for miles, and they had men post-ed in trees, who could not be seen, but could pick off the A-mer-i-cans one by one as they came on.

One of the worst parts of the fight was at El Ca-ney, a place four miles from the north end of the city. There the Span-iards had one stone and one brick fort, and four log block-houses set in banks of earth. These works were so placed that they could pour a cross-fire on a force that should come from east or west. They had deep trench-es where food could be brought to those at work. At each open place in the woods that could be seen from the block-houses they had put up a large sheet of zinc, to serve as a guide for their shots, as these made a bright back-ground for troops that passed by. The fire from these block-houses was so fierce that the troops could not face it, and there was great loss of life. The men fought like he-

AD-MI-RAL CER-VE-RA.

roes, but they did not win till field-guns were brought. They had to push these guns through the mud and drag them up a steep hill, with the fire from the Span-ish on them all the time. Then the foe hid in the tops of leafy trees did sad work. They used pow-der that did not smoke, so the A-mer-i-cans could not see where the shots came from. A fierce sun beat on the men, that was hard to bear, and some were struck by it. The men's throats were so parched that they could scarce speak loud. The Rough Ri-ders, with Colo-nel Roose-velt at their head, and the 1st and the 10th climbed up the steep San Juan Hill in the face of such a fierce fire from the block-house that they paused once. Roose-velt saw it and dashed out. He yelled to his men to come on, and they did not stop long. They raced up with yells and shouts, but some fell and died with the cheers of their friends in their ears. Roose-velt's horse was shot, but he ran on to keep in the van. So the A-mer-i-cans won step by step till the ranks of the foe broke and they fled pell mell back to San-ti-a-go. The loss to the A-mer-i-cans was great, but they had won the day, and it seemed that San-ti-a-go must soon fall in-to the hands of the A-mer-i-cans. Gen-er-al Shaf-ter was at the head of the forces by land and Ad-mi-ral Samp-son led the force at sea.

On July 3d a cloud of smoke was seen in the bay, and the A-mer-i-cans saw that Ad-mi-ral Cer-ve-ra had made a bold dash to get out with his fleet. A cry went up from ship to ship of the A-mer-i-cans.

Men sprang to their guns, and the great war-ships start-ed to head off the Span-iards. They were fired on from the fleet and from Mor-ro Cas-tle. Shot and shell splashed in the waves. The whole surf seemed on fire. The fleet was hemmed in by fire. Some of the Spanish ships were on fire too, and their crews ran them on shore, so that they might save the lives of those who had been spared by the A-mer-i-can shells. At last the ship of Ad-mi-ral Cer-ve-ra was set on fire by the shells, but he changed his course and head-ed off for the coast as if he meant to run for it. But it was

COLO-NEL ROOSE-VELT.

too late. The A-mer-i-can ships gave chase, and he made for the rocks. They bore down on the doomed ship with full speed. She struck bow end on the rocks and rest-ed there. Red flames burst through the black smoke on her deck. The A-mer-i-cans stopped their fire and made for the boat. So the whole Span-ish fleet was wrecked and spoiled, and Ad-mi-ral Cer-ve-ra and twelve hun-dred Span-iards fell in-to the hands of the A-mer-i-cans.

Gen-er-al Shaf-ter sent word at once to the Span-ish Gen-er-al Tor-al, who was in charge of San-ti-a-go, that he must now give up the town. He told him that the Span-ish fleet was wrecked. He said that if he did not give up he would at once send shot and shell on the town and the gun-boats in the bay would help him. Gen-er-al Tor-al said he would give up if they would let him go free with all his troops. Gen-er-al Shaf-ter would not do this. So when the truce was at an end they fired once more. Gen-er-al Shaf-ter had his force laid out in such a way that there was no chance for the Span-iards to get off, for the A-mer-i-cans were on all sides of San-ti-a-go. Gen-er-al Miles with more troops joined them. The great guns were so placed that they could have dropped shells on the town at the rate of thir-ty in an hour. On the 10th of Ju-ly some ships of the fleet threw shells at the town, but they fell short and did no harm. The next day they got in range and the land force took part in the fight.

Once more Gen-er-al Shaf-ter called on Gen-er-al

The War with Spain. 243

Tor-al to give up the town, and said that his troops would be sent back to Spain by the U-ni-ted States.

To these terms Gen-er-al Tor-al saw fit to yield. On the 17th of Ju-ly, just as the church bell rang out the hour of twelve, the Flag of the Un-ion was flung out over the pal-ace of the Gov-er-nor. It was a clear day, and there was not a cloud in the blue sky. A vast crowd of folk were there. The band played and can-non boomed from the bay. In just four weeks from the time the A-mer-i-cans land-ed in Cu-ba San-ti-a-go had fall-en.

GEN-ER-AL MILES.

Por-to Ri-co is an isle not far from Cu-ba, and is said to be the gem of the group. The ground is so rich that fruits, sug-ar and cof-fee, flax, rice and maize grow with scarce any care. San Juan is the chief town. The folk of Por-to Ri-co were no more fond of the Span-iards than the folk of Cu-ba. Gen-er-al Miles took charge of the troops for Por-to Ri-co. Gun-boats were sent to Ponce, one of the chief towns, to ask that they should give up to the A-mer-i-cans. The folk met the troops with great joy. They cheered them in the streets and load-ed them with gifts. They were pleased to have the star-ry flag wave o-ver them. There is a road from Ponce to San Juan. As the troops of Gen-er-al Miles marched on, the Span-ish forces moved back to San Juan. At all points the folk met the A-mer-i-cans with glad words and cheers and praise. It seemed as if they wished with all their hearts to be friends.

There might have been a fight at Pa-blo Vas-ques with some Span-ish troops, for the guns were trained on the foe, but the news of peace came just in the nick of time.

Peace was signed on Au-gust the 12th. The terms were that Spain should give all claim and all rights to Cu-ba.

That Spain should give up to the A-mer-i-cans Por-to Ri-co and all the isles owned by Spain in the An-tilles, as well as one isle in the La-drones which the U-ni-ted States should choose.

That the U-ni-ted States should keep Ma-ni-la and its port.

That the Span-iards should leave all these places at a time fixed by the U-ni-ted States.

That Spain and the U-ni-ted States should each choose five men to meet in Par-is on Oc-to-ber 1st and talk of these terms and fix the fate of the Phil-ip-pines.

It takes some time for news to go from the U-ni-ted States to Ma-ni-la, so Ad-mi-ral Dew-ey had not heard of peace when he laid siege to that place. On Au-gust the 17th the ships by sea and the force by land drove out the Span-iards with the loss of but a few men on the A-mer-i-can side. The A-mer-i-can troops filed through the gates and the town was given up. The Span-iards formed in line and laid down their arms. Their loss in the trench-es had been great. The A-mer-i-can flag was once raised on the pal-ace.

Ma-ni-la is the chief town of the Phil-ip-pines, and lies on a bay so large and fine that it is said the ships of the world could find room there. There are six hun-dred isles in the Phil-ip-pines, but some are small. There is but one rail-road there, so you see Spain did not do much for the place. There are wild tribes who hat-ed Spain, and had armed and formed bands to fight the Span-iards. They were glad to have the A-mer-i-cans help them fight Spain, but they did not want them to stay. Some of them chose a Pres-i-dent whose name is A-guin-al-do, but some do not want him. So it seems as if some time must pass before peace comes to the Phil-ip-pines

On the 1st of Jan-u-ary, 1899, the flag of Spain which had waved over Cu-ba for 400 years was hauled down at Ha-van-a. The Stars and Stripes went up, and the crowds in the streets cheered till they were hoarse. Shouts of "Mc-Kin-ley" and "Free Cu-ba" rent the air.

Cu-ba is free. Her tears will flow no more. The dark night through which she fought with such a brave heart now gives place to the dawn of a new day. That isle—the pearl of the sea—may now shine once more in the light of peace. May she not cease to love the land that raised her from the dust and the "flag that made her free."

If you are interested in receiving a free catalog of other
Mantle Ministries' books, videos, and cassettes,
send a self-stamped addressed envelope to:
MANTLE MINISTRIES
228 Still Ridge
Bulverde, TEXAS 78163
or call:
OFFICE: 830-438-3777
FAX: 830-438-3370
E-MAIL: mantle3377@aol.com
HOME PAGE: http://www.mantlemin.com